ADOPTION
& FOSTERING

Learn the Child

Helping looked after children to learn

Kate Cairns and Chris Stanway

Published by
British Association for Adoption & Fostering
(BAAF)
Skyline House
200 Union Street
London SE1 0LX
www.baaf.org.uk

Charity registration 275689

© Kate Cairns and Chris Stanway, 2004

British Library Cataloguing in Publication Data
A catalogue record for this book is available from the British Library

ISBN 1 903699 38 X

Project management by Shaila Shah, Director of Publications, BAAF

Photographs on cover and in the book posed by models
by John Birdsall
www.johnbirdsall.co.uk

Designed by Andrew Haig & Associates

Printed by The Russell Press (TU) Nottingham

BAAF Adoption & Fostering is the leading UK-wide membership organisation for all
those concerned with adoption, fostering and child care issues.

Contents

Notes about the authors

Kate Cairns is a social worker and social work teacher. With her partner, Brian, and their three birth children she provided permanence for a group of twelve looked after children, all of whom are now adult. She was a family placement social worker for five years, and a trainer/consultant for BAAF for three years. She is the author of *Attachment, Trauma and Resilience: Therapeutic caring for children*.

Chris Stanway has been teaching in secondary education for 27 years. She has been a Head of Year, Head of Careers Guidance, and now works as a Special Educational Needs Co-ordinator and Assistant Headteacher in a Community Technology College serving a very diverse population. She is the designated teacher for looked after children in the school.

Acknowledgements

We would like to thank all the teachers in the 76 schools who took part in our survey. Particular thanks go to the teachers, educational social workers and others who gave time and thought to face-to-face follow-up interviews.

We would also like to thank all those from the ten fostering agencies, local authorities and other organisations that invited us to use some of this material in training and gave us invaluable feedback.

Introduction

> *The principal challenge in dealing with children in public care was identified as managing their challenging behaviour. There was good awareness that challenging behaviour arose from the young people's previous traumatic experiences, some of which might be known to the school, while other experiences (for example, those of asylum seekers) might only be guessed at. The forging of strong relationships with pupils causing concern so that the pupils knew that schools were prepared to support them was considered to be one of the most effective ways of addressing undesirable behaviour.*
>
> Fletcher-Campbell F, Archer T and Tomlinson K (2003) *The Role of the School in Supporting the Education of Children in Public Care*, National Foundation for Educational Research

This resource pack addresses itself to the greatest difficulty in the education of looked after children identified by teachers – the behaviour of the children themselves. It explains how, by giving attention to the special physiological, emotional and psychological needs of traumatised children, we can help them to manage themselves and to derive full benefit from their life at school. It also sets out the ways in which caring for traumatised children changes the thoughts and feelings of the adults around the child, and suggests a reflective and supervised practice that will ensure that everyone involved remains healthy and functions as well as possible.

This pack has been produced in response to many discussions with foster carers, social workers and teachers. Working as we have done for many years in teaching, social work and foster care, we wanted to provide material that would be useful to all these people in their work of supporting children in public care to achieve the best possible educational outcomes.

The pack consists of this book and a CD ROM containing a PowerPoint presentation and a set of handouts. The presentation can be used by anyone involved in the care and education of looked after children. It can be used as, or to contribute to, training material for any individuals or groups who would find it useful. The material is copyright, so it should not be used or copied for any commercial purposes. But it is intended to be used fully to help and inform work with children in public care.

The book is in three parts. The first part sets the context for the training material and provides some case studies constructed by current practitioners in schools to illustrate the complexity of the lives of the children with whom they work. The second part provides notes to accompany the PowerPoint presentation, commenting on any slides that may need clarifying. The third part suggests various ways in which the resource pack material could be used in training, supervision, and discussions. It also includes a list of key people involved in the education of looked after children, and a list of useful books.

Children in public care represent a very small proportion of the child population. One frequent comment when this material was being developed and piloted was that these ideas apply to *all* traumatised children. The training material could therefore be used in many areas of education and social care.

There are a number of useful resource and practice guides supporting improvements in educational outcomes for children and young people looked after in public care (see at the back of this book for full details). These include:

- *Education Matters: For everyone working with children in public care* produced by The Who Cares? Trust

- The Social Exclusion Unit practice guide *A Better Education for Children in Care*

- *Education: A carer's handbook* produced by the National Teaching and Advisory Service

- *The Role of the School in Supporting the Education of Children in Public Care* produced by the DfES.

These guides are essential items for the bookshelves, and the day-to-day practice, of teachers, carers and social workers. They give overviews of the systems that currently provide for the educational needs of children looked after in public care, and examples of best practice. The guides also offer models for structural changes that may enhance the educational attainment of looked after children.

This resource pack is an addition to, and not a replacement for, the existing literature. It is based on the observation, drawn from many years experience in teaching and in foster care, that structural changes on their own will not solve the educational difficulties of many looked after children and young people. We find ourselves working from the premise that even if (and when) all other things are equal in the education of looked after children, something else is going on. We notice that children in public care often struggle more than their peers to manage in school. And we also notice that the responsible adults around looked after children often behave differently from the way they behave in dealing with other children.

The material provided in this book and CD ROM offers a model for making sense of these observations. It suggests an approach that draws on our knowledge and understanding of the long-term effects of trauma in childhood. It also offers practical guidance, based on this model, for supporting the education of looked after children.

Part 1
Overview

1
2
3

What we already know

- There are about 55,000 children and young people in public care.

- This is about 0.5 per cent of the child population.

- Most of these children have a history of family breakdown, or neglect, or abuse, or rejection, or a combination of these.

- All these children have suffered separation from their families and have experienced significant loss in their lives.

- Many of these children experience multiple moves both before and during their time of being looked after.

- The number of looked after children in any individual school is usually very small. Many schools have no children in public care.

- Looked after children do less well then their peers at all stages of education.

- Their underachievement becomes progressively worse as they get older.

- In 2001, only 50 per cent achieved one GCSE at grade A–G, as against 96 per cent of the peer population as a whole.

- In the same year only 8 per cent achieved 5 GCSE passes at Grades A–C, as against 48 per cent of the whole peer population.

- Looked after children are nine times more likely than their peers to have a statement of special educational need.

- They are 13 times more likely to be permanently excluded from school.

- They have a high incidence of missed days of schooling.

- Research carried out for the Department for Education and Skills (DfES) by Felicity Fletcher-Campbell, Tamsin Archer and Kathryn Tomlinson and recorded in Research Report RR498 (*The Role of the School in Supporting the Education of Children in Public Care*) shows that teachers find challenging behaviour the principal difficulty in dealing with children in public care (Fletcher-Campbell *et al*, 2003).

- The difficulty, according to this research, is not a lack of understanding of the origins of the behaviour, but of finding ways to deal with such behaviour in the context of running a school.

What should happen

- There have been around 22 major legislative Acts in England and Wales since 1989, with the Green Paper, *Every Child Matters* (DfES, 2003), heralding further change. Since 1999, 17 major reports have been published, each of which provides valuable insights into the issues and give examples of good practice.

- Schools give the chance for young people to grow, to expand their knowledge, to have the courage to dream, learn to be unafraid to fail, to gain qualifications, to forge friendships, to be part of society, to meet with adults who care, to rebel within safe limits, to meet with people unlike themselves. They can 'boost a child's health through raising self-confidence and self-esteem, enabling participation in sports and giving access to health education' (Social Exclusion Unit, 2003)

- Schools can also be places where, if you don't belong, you can feel isolated and alone, get picked on for being different, feel lost.

- The joint inspection report, *Education of children who are looked after by local authorities* (SSI/Ofsted, 1994) concluded:

  > *If the standards of achievement of the children are to be improved, individual schools have to assume, in conjunction with the LEA, a greater responsibility for fostering and maintaining the partnership with social services and developing strategies which promote the achievements of children.*

- The *Review of the Safeguards for Children Living Away from Home* undertaken by Sir William Utting in 1996 led to

- *People Like us* (Utting, 1997) which noted:

  > *Education plays a critical part in the "welfare" of looked after children who continue to underachieve in educational terms.*

- The *Government Response to Children's Safeguards Review* (Department of Health, 1998) stated that:

  > *The Government is convinced that the quality of the public care system in which children are looked after by local authorities is unacceptably low.*

- *Quality Protects* (Department of Health, 1998) (England only) is a five-year programme to overhaul children's services with 11 national objectives, and £885 million "new money" to support the initiatives.

  > *To ensure that children looked after gain maximum life chance benefits from educational opportunities (Objective 4).*

- *Truancy and School Exclusion* (Social Exclusion Unit, 1998) an early report, noted that:

  > *Effective education should be considered a key outcome of relevant social services work.*

and aimed to:

> *... reduce by one third the numbers of permanent, fixed term exclusions and time lost to truancy by 2002.*

- Later that year, the Department of Health set educational targets in their *National Priorities Guidance* (Department of Health, 1998) which was enshrined in the School Standards Act (see below) including:

> *To improve the educational attainment by increasing to at least 50% by 2001 the proportion of children leaving care at 16 or later with a GCSE or GNVQ qualification increasing to 75% by 2003.*

- The School Standards and Framework Act 1998 included some specific references to the education of looked after children:

  - Local education authorities are required to include National Priorities guidance within new Education Development Plans

  - New "Standard Funds" were introduced (specifically Social Inclusion: Pupil Support Grant 19), with some money protected by government each year for use in education of looked after children initiatives.

- The *Joint Guidance on the Education of Children in Public Care* (DH/DfES, 2000) stresses the importance of having high expectations for looked after children. The introduction states:

> *For too long the education of young people in public care has been characterised by fragmentation and unacceptable levels of failure. The underachievement of children in public care, and the failure of agencies to work together in meeting their needs, is well documented ... leaving care statistics reveal unacceptable levels of underachievement: 75 per cent of care leavers leave formal education with no qualifications, and between 12 per cent and 19 per cent go on to further education compared with 68 per cent of the general population. Action is now urgently required to improve the quality of corporate parenting and the educational experiences and achievements of children in residential and foster care.*

- The National Minimum Standards for Children's Homes and Fostering Services (Department of Health, 2002) also covers important areas.

- The report, *A Better Education for Children in Care* (Social Exclusion Unit, 2003), was commissioned to examine what needs to be done in order to improve the education of looked after children. Five key issues were identified:

> *Too many young people's lives are characterised by instability.*

> *Young people in care spend too much time out of school or other place of learning.*

> *Children do not have sufficient help with their education if they get behind.*

Carers are not expected, or equipped, to provide sufficient support and encouragement at home for learning and development.

Children in care need more help with their emotional, mental or physical health and well-being.

- The Green Paper, *Every Child Matters* (DfES, 2003), sets out proposals for a framework for improving outcomes for all children and their families. This is to happen by a radical re-thinking of the way children's services are planned and delivered. The aim is to create a seamless service to all children by the creation of Children's Trusts by 2006. These Trusts will be integrated teams of health and education professionals, social workers and Connexions advisors based in and around schools and children's centres. It also enshrines a new duty on local authorities to promote the educational attainment of looked after children.

- Research has clearly been indicating that children in public care generally enter adult life having achieved much less educationally than their peers. It has also been demonstrated that educational achievement is a critical factor in developing the resilience that will serve as a resource throughout life.

- Social policy has clearly followed these research findings. Solutions have been proposed, and sometimes, in some places, implemented. Yet there are tensions involved in these very solutions, tensions that reduce the effectiveness of implementation of measures, and reduce the effectiveness of the measures when implemented.

- These tensions were clearly indicated in the findings of a survey of opinion (conducted by the authors) among all the designated teachers for looked after children in one local authority in a shire county. Points raised include the following:

  - Services for children are diverse and very different from each other in both form and content. Attempts to integrate such services often, paradoxically, lead to changes that focus on the services and there is a loss of focus on the needs of the child.

  - Attempts to establish standards to ensure that the needs of children are met can lead to centralisation of control. This reduces local autonomy which reduces local accountability and can devalue local initiatives. Workers can then feel powerless and demoralised.

  - If schools are seen as the centre for resolving the educational difficulties of children in public care – a tiny minority of the school population – this is at odds with other educational imperatives to focus on narrow ranges of attainment.

What do practitioners think should happen?

The survey of opinion (conducted by the authors) of secondary school designated teachers for looked after children within a large local authority highlighted some key issues of concern. We are confident that these concerns are widespread, and can be summarised under three headings:

Communication

- Maintaining effective and regular dialogue between agencies can be difficult. There need to be clear pathways established so that understanding about the differing pressures can be improved. It can appear that communication with schools about placements is a low priority for social services so information that could help schools better understand the needs of the child is not shared. This is particularly worrying when there is lack of information about changes in placements.

- The implementation of the "designated teacher" role is improving the quality of liaison and this is also enhanced by the appointment of Education Support Workers who can provide a consistent link within local social services departments.

Co-ordination

- The number, purpose and quality of meetings about individual children is a source of concern to schools. There can appear to be a great deal of duplication of effort and information.

- The completion of Personal Education Plans (PEPs) can help to clarify responsibilities although these need to be reviewed regularly if they are to be effective.

Training

- Joint training between education and social services departments is a priority. Where area group meetings are established they are very successful in disseminating good practice. However, because the numbers of looked after children in any one school tend to be low, funding for such training from school budgets can be problematic. If quality of provision is to be improved nationally, there needs to be a co-ordinated and centrally funded programme of training.

These themes also emerged from a series of focus group discussions with foster carers and social workers. The group discussions also revealed the need for high quality support for care families, and this became a further identified theme.

Support for care families

● **Supervision**: carers and social workers who had taken part in training on the impact of living with traumatised children were aware of the need for the family to be supervised by knowledgeable and skilled people who could address all the issues.

● **Respite care**: regular and occasional respite tailored to the unique situation of the care family and adaptable to changing circumstances was seen as a resource that was needed as part of the placement arrangement, rather than as a last resort when families were exhausted.

● **School liaison**: families sometimes needed professional liaison and mediation with schools and local education authorities (LEAs) in order to achieve the best educational outcome for the child in their care

● **Therapy**: traumatised children need a range of therapeutic options to be available at different points in their recovery process. Members of the care family could also benefit from therapy at times.

1

Case studies

We asked teachers accustomed to working with looked after children to contribute to case studies that would be composite, and would adequately portray without exaggeration the complexity of the lives of children in public care at this point of the 21st century. Out of these ideas we produced six composite case studies.

POSED BY MODEL

1 Susan
A 16-year-old girl

Susan is 16 years old. She is of mixed heritage and has been on a care order since she was two. Her mother works as a prostitute in a large city; she is a heroin user who has been in and out of rehabilitation units and prison on a regular basis since before Susan was born.

As a young child Susan was extremely withdrawn with significant speech delay. Between the ages of two and seven she was placed with a succession of local authority foster carers but each placement broke down within two months because she would not communicate, consistently soiled herself and her surroundings and was aggressive towards other children in the home. When she was with her mother, Susan displayed none of these characteristics, and indeed appeared to thrive – except that all school attendance stopped. She was placed on the Child Protection Register and regular social service visits were made to the home.

When Susan was eight, her mother was imprisoned for a 12-month sentence for GBH, drug dealing and soliciting. Susan went into a local authority children's home and started attending junior school regularly. She was compliant with all school procedures but very withdrawn, rarely offering any information. Despite this, she made rapid academic progress with literacy and numeracy skills and cognitive testing confirmed that she was potentially very able. During this time she disclosed that she had been subject to sexual abuse from a series of men while she had been living with her mother. Susan felt that this had helped her mother and made Susan herself feel grown up.

After her mother was released from prison, Susan started persistently running away from the home in order to be with her.

At age ten, Susan was placed out of county with an independent fostering provider. She initially appeared to settle well, but after six months she stopped eating and had to be hospitalised. Exhaustive counselling and therapy by mental health workers followed and Susan slowly began to thrive once more. There followed a period of settled calm, her mother was once again imprisoned and Susan was regularly in a school that she enjoyed.

At puberty Susan underwent a sudden and cataclysmic change. Her behaviour in the home and at school became aggressive and she physically attacked a younger girl. She was excluded from school and ran back to the city to be with her mother. She refused to leave and had to be physically restrained. Her mother at this point said that she didn't want anything more to do with Susan and that she was nothing but trouble.

Susan was placed with a new fostering agency and moved to a different part of the country. She refused to attend school and became clinically depressed – not talking, sleeping throughout the day, refusing to leave her room, cutting her legs and arms, binge eating so that she gained a huge amount of weight, and obsessively washing her hair.

This foster carer, however, refused to give up and after six months of careful work, using resources from many agencies, Susan agreed to begin an integration programme into a local secondary school supported by the Pupil Referral Unit (PRU) where she had made some positive relationships with staff.

She started with one subject, English. She found it difficult to stay in a classroom for a whole hour so was allowed to leave with a support worker, at any time. Her attitude towards teachers was often confrontational and she would abscond frequently from the school site. She would constantly challenge rules but all staff were aware of her problems and had agreed clear responses.

She was in the school for three years and in the end passed GCSEs in five subjects, gaining high grades in Art and English. The day she was due to start sixth form studies she received a text message from her mother and returned to live with her.

POSED BY MODEL

2 Andy
A 12-year-old boy

Andy was diagnosed with Attention Deficit Hyperactivity Disorder (ADHD) when he was eight years old. This was three years after his father had left home, after which his mother had moved her female partner and her partner's three-year-old daughter into the family home.

The diagnosis was arrived at during an assessment process after Andy had been permanently excluded from his junior school, and had been cautioned by police for taking and driving away a car and for sexually interfering with his young stepsister. He was taken into care and placed with local authority foster carers.

There was no full-time education available to provide for his needs, but Andy was provided with half-time schooling at a local PRU. Within two weeks Andy had set fire to the building, causing the unit to close. At home he was not sleeping and was prescribed low dose sleeping pills as well as Ritalin for control of the ADHD. The foster placement rapidly broke down when it was discovered that Andy was being overtly sexual towards another child within the home.

Andy was then placed in a children's home in a different area and integrated into a new junior school. He rapidly got into trouble with the police for setting fires and he returned under supervision to his mother's house as she was now living alone. There followed a period where Andy was in constant trouble with the law. He was vandalising the estate, putting lit fireworks through neighbours doors, setting vehicles on fire and drinking alcohol stolen from his own and other people's houses. He was finally taken back into foster care after assaulting his mother with a broken bottle. During this time, he did not receive any formal education, as no school would accept him on roll.

Transfer to secondary phase education took place with massive co-operation between the school and the local PRU. Statutory assessment procedures were started with the intention of providing Andy with a Statement of Special Educational Needs (SEN) as a result of his extremely challenging behaviour.

Three foster family placements broke down over a three-month period, with Andy causing damage to property in each place. Consistent schooling was maintained, however, with Andy being taxied in to school from wherever he was placed in the local authority area. During the school holiday he ran away from his foster placement and returned to his mother. She could not persuade him to leave the house, and therefore she moved out herself to stay with friends. Alone in the house, he trashed the building and was taken into secure accommodation.

He started the new term as a five-day boarder in a special school for children with Emotional and Behavioural Difficulties (EBD). With weekends spent in a children's home and secure boarding during the week, Andy survived and even flourished in this protected environment for two terms. On the last day of term he set fire to the school and at the age of 12 he was transferred to a detention centre.

POSED BY MODEL

3 Gita

A 14-year-old girl

Now 14, Gita is the second of four children, each of whom has a different father. Gita's mother is of mixed Hindu Indian and white British heritage and grew up in care herself. Her father, whom Gita has never met, is said by her mother to be Pakistani. When Gita was seven, her mother formed her first long-term relationship with a man who moved into the family home as stepfather to the children.

He was racist and physically abusive to Gita and her sister, whose father is African-Caribbean. All four children were made subject to a care order and accommodated when Gita was eight. She spent time in two children's homes and five foster placements over the following three years. The final two placements broke down because of her violent behaviour towards younger children in the home. These changes of placement involved her in attending four different primary schools. There is no record of her ever taking Standard Attainment Tests (SATs) at Key Stages 1 and 2.

In the summer, when she was 11, Gita's stepfather was found dead in his lodgings. Gita returned home to live with her mother and started attending the local secondary school. Within three months, she was on the verge of being permanently excluded for repeated violent attacks on her peers who, she claimed, were taunting her, saying she had had sex with her dead stepfather.

Meanwhile, all her siblings remained in local authority care and, at her mother's request, Gita was taken back to a new foster placement. She was admitted to a new secondary school. Within two weeks she had run away from the placement and was returned to a children's home.

Her attitude at school was initially polite and compliant. She showed quick interest in a variety of subjects, although testing revealed that her literacy and numeracy skills were two years below her chronological age. In her second week at the new school, Gita physically attacked a girl on the way to school. Gita claimed that the girl had been teasing her about her stepfather. She was excluded for five days and an interagency meeting was called. As a result of this, Gita was offered bereavement counselling and a psychological assessment from the Adolescent Mental Health Team.

On her return to school, a protracted battle began to get Gita to go into classrooms. She would start off in a lesson, be apparently working well and then suddenly down tools and leave, often swearing loudly as she went. She would then hide herself under stairs, in toilets, or behind cupboards and wait to be found. At first she would then return quietly to class for the rest of the day, but over a period of a month or so, her reaction to staff finding her became increasingly abusive. Finally, she would no longer return at all but instead walked off around the site.

A staff meeting decided to adopt a whole school policy of not reacting to this, but if Gita was seen out of class she would be asked in a non-confrontational manner to report herself to the support base. She started to stay in classes for whole days.

After three weeks, Gita suddenly stopped attending and the school could not discover her whereabouts. Enquiries revealed that she had been moved out of the area and placed in a foster home at the other end of the county. After six weeks she re-appeared, having run away and returned to her mother's house. Despite the efforts of police and social workers, Gita refused to return to the foster placement and her mother agreed that she could stay at home 'as long as she behaved'. Gita now refused to attend any lessons, ran away from school, was caught on CCTV camera stealing from an office, and was verbally abusive to staff. The school referred her to the local Referral Unit for non-attending pupils (PRU).

Over the next year, Gita committed a series of acts of vandalism around the neighbourhood and was violent towards her younger siblings, causing one of them to be hospitalised. She was physically and verbally abusive to staff at the PRU and her mother freely admitted that Gita was beyond her control. The Young Offenders Team organised a variety of different programmes, but Gita never completed any of them.

Gita was included on an NVQ course in Catering but when she thought she might have to show her hands (which were discoloured with bruises and raw from biting), she ran away. She is now excluded from the PRU and is ten weeks pregnant.

POSED BY MODEL

4 John
A 12-year-old boy

John is 12 years old, and is the youngest of four children. The family have been known to social services since the birth of the first child, as the mother is a registered drug user and alcoholic. Their maternal grandmother took on responsibility for maintaining the home as best she could until she became too frail six years ago when John was six years old. When grandmother moved into sheltered housing the family home quickly deteriorated. The children's always sporadic school attendance now stopped completely and a protracted period of frustration for education welfare services and social services ensued. After some six months, entry was forced and inspection revealed the house to be in a state of foul neglect with the children malnourished and infested with lice. Remains of a birthday meal of baked beans was in evidence. Their mother was sectioned under the Mental Health Act and the children were placed in three different foster placements. John and his closest in age sister, who has severe learning difficulties, were separated for the first time.

The two elder girls lived together and went to school together but John went alone to his neighbourhood school. While the placements were stable for his siblings, John had problems settling and he developed speech and language difficulties, which manifested themselves as severe stuttering. He found it very difficult to make any significant friendships with peers and was frequently bullied. He withdrew from contact and would spend much of his time at school in tears, making contact only with his education liaison social worker. He was the only one of the children who refused to visit his grandmother, and he cut himself off from family contact.

John was assessed as having complex special educational needs with particular weakness in literacy and organisational skills. No SEN statement was, however, considered necessary.

It was difficult to persuade John to attend school and when he was on site he would often truant from lessons and be found hidden in small spaces. He started to steal from school staff and his carers. Two placements broke down because of the difficulties arising from his challenging behaviour.

When he was 11, John was placed with new carers, with a placement contract providing considerable extra educational input. He was given a place on an out-of-hours "reading for life" scheme run through social services in collaboration with the school; this provides John with access to a computer to use at home. He also has considerable time input from speech therapist. His latest foster placement is in walking distance from his sisters, and he is to join them in attending the same secondary school next year. He has made one visit to see his grandmother. John is beginning to respond positively to this integrated approach to his complex needs.

POSED BY MODEL

5 Wayne

A 13-year-old boy

Wayne is a highly intelligent 13-year-old. He is an only child who lived with his mother and her partner until the age of five. At that point his father lost his job and left the family home. His mother started drinking heavily and three months later also lost her well-paid job as a secretary in a large firm. She became mentally ill, suffering from prolonged bouts of severe depression during which she self-harmed. When Wayne was seven, his mother attempted suicide and was found unconscious in a pool of blood by her son when he returned from school one afternoon. He called the emergency services and her life was saved. He was taken into emergency care and placed in a children's home. He stayed there for six weeks but returned home when his mother was discharged from the psychiatric unit.

For a further year, Wayne lived at home where he took on many care responsibilities. The house was kept quite clean and tidy, clothes were washed, food prepared and bills paid. During the course of the year, the family social worker noted that Wayne was often at home when she called and the mother would say that the boy had been unwell. At the same time the school had referred Wayne to the education welfare service for erratic attendance and the school medical service registered concern about the boy's slow growth rate. Wayne's teacher noted that academic progress had practically stopped. It was not, however, until a multi-agency meeting was convened that the bits of the jigsaw fell into place.

It was agreed that Wayne should be taken into care and he was placed in an assessment centre. Full investigation of the home circumstances revealed that Wayne's mother was still drinking heavily and admitted that she was not able to cope with looking after herself and certainly not with looking after a child.

Wayne was placed with foster carers with weekly-supervised visits to his mother. School attendance improved dramatically and he began to resume normal growth patterns. He achieved Level 5 in Key Stage 2 tests – above the national average. His foster family reported that he was well settled in the home and got on well with their two daughters, both younger than Wayne. He was told this would be a permanent placement.

Wayne settled quickly into secondary school and presented as a quiet and likeable youngster, eager to please and well organised. He made good academic progress and was placed in high sets for all subjects.

In the summer holidays at the end of Year 7, Wayne spent some time with his father who had re-married and had a ten-month-old baby. When he returned at the start of Year 8, aged 12, staff noticed that he was quite uncommunicative. He stopped attending the after-school technology clubs he had enjoyed the previous year and his homework record became very poor. He had had a growth spurt and became clumsy and unco-ordinated. He developed a mild stammer and often refused to take part in PE lessons. Sometimes during afternoon lessons he appeared drowsy.

There were a couple of incidents of absences where Wayne produced forged sickness notes and alcohol was smelt on his breath. One day, another pupil reported that he had seen Wayne taking some tablets. He was found in a disorientated state in the cloakrooms and taken to the accident and emergency department of the local hospital having taken 15 paracetamol tablets.

Wayne's foster father came to a review meeting saying that his wife would not attend as she felt she had nothing positive to say about Wayne. Her two girls had revealed that they were now very nervous around Wayne and she herself felt that she could no longer talk to him. Wayne would not volunteer any information about what he was doing, just staring at her silently when she spoke to him. When she had grounded him in an attempt to manage his risky behaviour, he had climbed out of his bedroom window and been gone some hours.

The foster placement broke down and Wayne was placed in a children's home. Wayne's behaviour continues to cause concerns over his health and safety. His attendance at school has dropped to about 50 per cent.

POSED BY MODEL

6 Kayleigh
A 10-year-old girl

Kayleigh is ten and at present in year 6 at primary school. Her mother died suddenly when she was three, and she has clear memories of this event and how it affected her father. She was considered at risk of physical abuse from her older sister and taken in to foster care. She was an aggressive child and three foster placements broke down in quick succession.

Finding a family able to offer long-term security proved difficult but a placement was secured when Kayleigh was five which looked promising. She started school and made quick progress although she found it difficult to make friends and would often take things from others and protest loudly if challenged. She would bite and slap her peers who avoided contact with her. She grew quickly and was the tallest in her class. She tends to be clumsy and has a moderately severe hearing loss which was not recognised until she was seven years old.

In the foster home she got on very well with an older child, and was devastated when she was killed in a road accident. This contributed to a further period of difficult behaviour with many incidents of soiling and bedwetting. She was excluded from school and again had to be found a new kinship foster placement with an aunt.

Having moved in with her aunt, Kayleigh began to be more settled until an uncle re-appeared in the house having served a prison sentence. Kayleigh was considered to be at real risk of sexual abuse from this man and had to be removed.

At the age of nine, and in her third junior school in another district, Kayleigh again enjoyed some stability in her fifth foster placement. But by this stage her behaviour in school was proving extremely difficult to manage. She was seeing support workers from social services weekly and having considerable input from the behaviour support team in an attempt to provide some sustained schooling.

She complained regularly of being bullied by children at school and had no friends. Parents of other children complained that she was frightening their children by her "strange" behaviour and aggressive attitude. The school initiated statutory assessment with a view to providing Kayleigh with a Statement of SEN, but this was rejected by the local authority for lack of clear evidence. She was prescribed anti-depressants.

When she was just ten, her father committed suicide and Kayleigh was hospitalised for three months having broken her arm when she pulled furniture down on herself during a tantrum.

At present, social services are seeking a new foster placement for Kayleigh, and it is recommended that she attend a special school for children with emotional and behavioural difficulties when she reaches secondary school age.

Part 2

Supporting the education of looked after children

A PowerPoint presentation

How to use this PowerPoint presentation

1   Introducing the presentation material

The CD ROM that accompanies this book contains a PowerPoint presentation that can be used for a range of training purposes. The presentation is in three sections. The first section, *The Child*, provides a model for making sense of the disordered behaviour that can harm the educational attainment of traumatised children. The second section, *The Adults*, explores the ways in which the behaviour of adults can be affected by secondary traumatic stress when living and working with traumatised children. And the third section, *What you can do*, provides a model for effective action. Each of these sections can be used as a presentation in its own right.

Notes are provided for each of the slides in the presentation, with the exception of a few that seem self-explanatory. The notes are intended to amplify and clarify the presentation material. The presentation and notes can also be read as a text in themselves.

The CD ROM also contains a handout version of the presentation that can be used to produce overhead projector transparencies and handouts. In addition, the case studies are included as handouts, with notes for ways in which they can be used to promote and support discussion. When designing any training event on this subject, any of this material can be used in different combinations to create the training that most meets the needs of the groups or individuals involved. More ideas on how to use this material creatively are provided in Part 3 of this book.

powerpoint slide 1

Supporting the education of looked after children

What do looked after children have in common?

- **They are separated from their parents**
- **The separation involves trauma**
- **They are likely to underachieve at school**

- **Other common factors may include:**
  - adverse experience in infancy
  - history of traumatic experience
  - continuing stress in relation to contact with absent family members

The statistics are grim. The Department of Health national statistics drawn from OC2 Returns (Outcome Indicators for Looked after Children) show that these children consistently do much worse in primary and secondary education than their peers, and far fewer of them progress to further and higher education. Looked after children do worse than their exact peers, not merely worse than the national average. Even taking into account their prior history before coming into care, they seem to be additionally disadvantaged by being looked after. It is therefore important to think about what characterises their lives that makes them different from their peers.

The most obvious life factor shared by looked after children is that they have been separated from their parents. This will have been for good reasons. If they are lucky, it will be because their family network is currently unable to meet their needs, but has previously been able to do so. If they are less lucky, the separation will have come at the end of a long period of neglect or other maltreatment. In any case, the separation from all that has been familiar will be traumatic.

Thinking about looked after children as traumatised children allows us to develop a model that works with the individual child. It requires us to work out what, if anything, is more difficult for this child than their peers. When we know what this particular child finds difficult as a result of stress injuries, we can find ways to enable them to adapt and thrive. This also allows for the fact that every child recovers differently from injury. Some children do not carry any additional burdens through life as a consequence of trauma; others never fully recover from their childhood experience.

Once they are in care, it is likely that looked after children will experience continuing stress in relation to contact with absent family members. It is hard enough to set up working contact arrangements when parents separate or divorce, and it is much harder when the child is living outside their family. There is no such thing as a pain free contact arrangement. If children do not see their attachment figures, they grieve and may form idealised fantasies that cause problems. If they do see them, they still grieve and may also be retraumatised if the prior relationship was in any way abusive.

SECTION 1
The child

2

> **powerpoint slide 3**
>
> ## Why is it more difficult for looked after children to manage school life?
>
> - **They may experience many moves**
> - **They have to cope with profound changes in their living environment**
> - **They may suffer symptoms of Post-Traumatic Stress Disorder (PTSD)**
> - **They may have experienced developmental impairment as a result of maltreatment in infancy**

When adults move home, they experience disruption and often find the transition very stressful. Children are usually much more affected by transitions, especially transitions that separate them from their attachment figures. It is a perverse but inevitable fact that, the more traumatised the child, the more likely that they will experience multiple moves when in care. Troubled children are more difficult to care for and more difficult to manage in a mainstream environment than their less burdened peers.

Every child separated from their parents has to make massive attempts to learn and adapt to their new circumstances. It is almost impossible for us to conceive of the effect on young minds of being uprooted and replanted in an alien environment unless we have experienced this ourselves. Every aspect of life, every element of sensory experience, is transformed. It is not surprising that children's literature is full of such astonishing disruptions, for children have always been powerless and subject to the whims of an often unpredictable adult world. We know that children must sometimes be cared for separately from their parents, but for the child the first impact of the change is one of total dislocation.

Most children, most of the time, recover spontaneously from traumatic experience. For them to do so, three conditions must be met. They must have safety, they must be able to express what has happened to them, and they must be part of a secure social network with well-formed attachment relationships. It is clear that looked after children are least likely to recover spontaneously from the traumatic disruption of their lives. If the child is unable to recover from trauma, they are likely to develop symptoms of Post-Traumatic Stress Disorder (PTSD).

Some looked after children will have also lived through significant adverse experience in their very early lives. It is now known that early adversity can have profound and lasting effects on global development. When children have suffered such impairment of development, they are less able to recover from later traumatic experience. This is the "double whammy" faced by many children in public care.

Traumatic stress

- **The automatic response to trauma involves the production of toxic amounts of stress hormones which affect:**
  - brain function
  - all major body systems
  - social functioning

- **A *bio-psycho-social* injury**

Trauma is a Greek word meaning injury. Psychological trauma leading to mental disorder is defined as:

> *An event which is, or is realistically perceived to be, threatening to the life or personal integrity of self or others.*

and

> *– the reaction is one of fear, helplessness or horror.*

When subject to such terrifying experience, the human brain goes into survival mode. Injury is accepted as a trade for life. For children, separation from the primary attachment figure and familiar environment presents an overwhelming threat. This is true even when the attachment figure or the known environment is a source of harm. It is also true whether or not the parent has chosen the separation and relocation.

In response to such overwhelming threat, the brain floods the body with massive quantities of stress hormones. These cause major areas of brain function to close down, and others to become activated and sensitised. Anything that slows down response time, such as feelings, empathy, memory, rational thought, or reflectivity is turned off. Oxygen intake increases, and breathing and heart rate speed up. The long muscles become tense in preparation for flight or fight. Automatic activities such as digestion slow down or stop. Social awareness changes in survival mode, others being seen as threats or as means to an end. If spontaneous recovery is not possible, these global changes of function persist and affect all future development.

These injuries are truly global in their effects.

Lasting effects of traumatic stress injuries

- **Children who have lived through traumatic stress may experience functional impairment as a result**
- **The impairment is the result of the bio-psycho-social injury**
- **Such impairment is global in its effects**
- **It can occur in children with no prior impairment**
- **The effects are more complex and persistent in children with prior developmental impairment**

The key thing to remember with trauma is that it is injury. The child is injured as a result of the toxic mix and quantity of chemicals automatically generated in response to overwhelming threat. The lasting effects of any injury can never be deterministic. Too many unique factors contribute to the outcome. For any given child the best that can be said is that there is a certain statistical probability that they will suffer lasting impairment as a result of the stress injury. It is clear that every child is unique, both in terms of the exact nature of their experience of the world so far, and in terms of their responses to that experience.

Unfortunately the child whose circumstances prevent spontaneous recovery from traumatic stress injuries will suffer some measure of impairment. The nature and extent of the impairment will depend on complex resilience factors. The child will, nevertheless, adapt. Adaptation is the recourse of organisms unable to recover, and humans are particularly good at it. Adapting to persistent impairments after traumatic stress injuries, however, often leads to behaviours and other symptoms of disorder that are deeply puzzling to the rest of the world. Since stress is a whole organism response, the effects of impairments resulting from stress injuries are global. Every aspect of daily functioning may be affected. This can have a great impact on the ability of the child to manage themselves in the school environment.

Traumatic stress injuries affect everyone subject to overwhelming threat. Children whose previous history has been untroubled will still be affected by the stress of separation from primary attachment figures. When children have a prior history of developmental harm, however, the impact of the overwhelming stress is increased.

Examples of functional impairment

- **Effects on brain development and function**
- **Physiological effects**
- **Physical effects**
- **Emotional effects**
- **Social effects**

The brain is affected by stress disorders because key areas of brain function close down in response to overwhelming stress. Oxygen supply to these specific brain areas is reduced in response to trauma. If the stress continues, either because the person continues to be traumatised or because they are unable to recover, then those areas of the brain will reduce in volume. Children who have been subject to such trauma may have significant reductions in volume in those areas of the brain. As well as the impact on brain development of the traumatic events that lead to and surround the child being separated from their parents, some looked after children have previously suffered developmental impairment as a result of maltreatment in infancy. These children would already have reduced volume in these areas of the brain, and will be additionally impaired in their capacity to recover from and adapt to traumatic stress.

Physiologically the inner state of traumatised people is one of terror. This does not abate, but the child adapts to accommodate this highly aroused state as their normality. Children may remain hyperaroused, and exhibit a range of extreme behaviours indicative of the discomfort caused by their condition. Or they may dissociate in response to their physiological arousal. Dissociation is the capacity human beings have to split awareness. Being creatures of very large brain, we need the ability to filter our experience. Otherwise we would all be as overwhelmed as autistic and schizophrenic people, who have such difficulty in filtering and processing raw sensory experience.

The physical state of people living through overwhelming stress is highly disordered. The physiological arousal affects all our major organs, including heart, lungs, excretory organs, reproductive organs, and the skin. It also affects the way our senses work, and the state of our muscles and bones. It is exhausting to live with this degree of physical disorder.

Awareness of our own emotions, sensitivity to the emotions of others, and the capacity to put feelings into words, and therefore to process them, are all affected by traumatic stress. The traumatised child will be likely to experience emotional numbing and an inability to connect to feelings. When feelings do occur the child is not able to process the experience through language, so that the physiological changes of affective experience remain in the body. This retention in the body, or somatisation, of emotion leads to various psychosomatic conditions. The child may have an asthma attack instead of feeling excited, or may have diarrhoea instead of feeling nervous.

Socially, the traumatised child is constrained by what has been called the "glass wall" of trauma. Cut off from others, preoccupied with trauma-related thoughts and feelings, unpredictably subject to panic or rage, unable to explain their actions or engage in moral accountability, these are often uncomfortable companions for those around them.

2

Effects on brain development and function

- **These functions may be diminished or lost:**
  - language, especially spoken language
  - words for feelings
  - sense of meaning and connection
  - empathy
  - impulse control
  - mood regulation
  - short-term memory
  - capacity for joy

Broca's Area, the part of the brain dealing with language as the spoken word, switches off in response to traumatic stress. Traumatised adults who were highly articulate before the trauma are likely to become much less able to communicate freely and expressively when in the grip of overwhelming stress. By how much more are children affected by this loss of coherent and articulate expression. This is particularly noticeable in relation to the expression of feelings. Another area of the brain, the hippocampus, normally acts as a map for the translation of emotions into words. This area also loses oxygen supply under the impact of trauma. It can become impossible for articulate and experienced adults even to find the word for a common affective state such as rage or disgust when in a state of traumatic stress. For children, the loss of inner state language and sensitivity is likely to be much more profound.

Our ability to create a sense of meaning and connection is also damaged or destroyed when we cannot make reliable links between our inner state and our sensory experience of the physical and social environment in which we live. This loss of meaning is one of the most profound consequences of disorders after trauma. Again, the implications for children, who are ordinarily busy forming their own unique sense of identity and meaning, are vast.

Traumatised people are likely to lose function in areas of the left prefrontal cortex dealing with empathy and impulse control. And the capacity for mood regulation is also likely to suffer harm. All these injuries can be persistent, and some research has indicated evidence of continuing brain injury in young adults traumatised as infants.

Memory is commonly disordered after trauma. Many people suffer either amnesia for the trauma, or hypermnesia, in which it is impossible to forget the traumatic events. These disorders make life difficult, but the short-term memory loss which is common after trauma is even more disabling day-to-day. Children living with stress injuries are often the children who never have the right kit at the right time in the right place. They simply cannot hold memory for long enough to make sense of a demanding environment.

Anhedonia, or the loss of the capacity for joy, has a deadening effect on daily life. Aesthetic delight and simple pleasure are keys to learning that are missing for traumatised children.

powerpoint slide 8

Physiological effects

- **Perpetual extreme levels of stress arousal may lead to:**
  - hypervigilance and loss of ability to concentrate
  - altered vision and hearing
  - hyperactivity or dissociation
  - avoidance of potential triggers to trauma
  - altered sleep patterns
  - altered eating patterns
  - compulsive self-harm
  - attempts to self-medicate with substances

Hypervigilance is the consequence in terms of attention of the perpetual state of stress arousal that follows unresolved trauma. Hypervigilant children can never relax. They are always alert for danger, and will perceive neutral stimuli as threatening. Although physiologically prepared for danger, they are in practice often poor at risk assessment, since if everything is dangerous then nothing is more dangerous than anything else. Attention and concentration are both severely reduced by hypervigilance. Children who cannot concentrate cannot learn.

Sensory fields change with hypervigilance. Peripheral vision is sharper, scanning the environment for threat, with the result that focused vision is diminished so that focused tasks such as reading quickly drift out of sight. Similarly the human ear usually gives preference to the human voice, so that people with no hearing impairment can usually pick out the voices of others even through considerable background sound. Hypervigilant children, however, live with their hearing permanently alert for sounds of danger and automatically tune out non-threatening sounds, so that they often fail to hear both information and instruction.

Some children remain hyperaroused, some children dissociate, and some children alternate between the two. It is important to notice children who dissociate, since their distress may be much less apparent than that of hyperaroused children. Physiologically their stress levels are just as high, and they are continuing to suffer harm even when it does not show.

Avoidance alternates with intrusive arousal in post-traumatic stress disorders. If the child were able to recover spontaneously, it would be the breathing space between periods of processing the trauma. For children unable to recover, avoidance leads to many problems. The avoidant person is unable to perceive that they are avoiding anything. Instead they feel frighteningly out of control, or they find reasons for their own behaviour that satisfy them and puzzle others. Avoidant children may avoid any aspect of daily life, since they will not distinguish realistic triggers from neutral stimuli. Particular lessons, or activities, or people, or times of day may all be avoided without the child being able to give a rationally satisfying explanation for their behaviour.

Children who sleep badly do poorly at school. Sleep disturbance is common after trauma. Children whose sleep is disrupted may suffer severe anxiety when they are in unfamiliar surroundings. Some children oversleep, or fall asleep inappropriately as a dissociation response in trigger situations. Many children suffer nightmares or night terrors when separated from their parents. These effects occur in children who previously had established patterns of regular sleep. Those who experienced early maltreatment may never have developed such ordered states of relaxation, and their disorder will be intensified.

Traumatised children may lose their appetite, or overeat for comfort, or lose any established patterns of eating. They may also crave high stimulus foods such as fizzy drinks and junk food.

Self-harm is a deeply worrying manifestation of stress disorders. The causes of self-harm after trauma are complex. Some children become addicted to the self-generated pain relievers that accompany traumatic stress and harm themselves to obtain a dose. Some develop a profound self-hatred as a consequence of traumatic stress capturing core elements of identity and destroying self-esteem. Some suffer from profound depression after trauma and may self-harm as an alternative to suicide. Some self-harm in an attempt to overcome the numbing and alienation from their own experience. Others who have been abused may internalise the aggressor and then become victim to their own aggression. The key to distinguishing between the many origins of self-harm after trauma is to take careful note of the messages from the child about their own perception of the self-harm. There is a great difference between the child who says: 'The only time I feel normal is when I cut myself', which speaks of addiction; 'I hate myself. I deserve to be hurt', which implies self-victimisation; 'I hate my life. I just want to die', which is related to suicide, and 'I just wanted to feel something', which may be related to the urge to live.

Traumatised children lack the capacity to regulate their own physiology. As they grow older this becomes ever more burdensome. They can also perceive that this inability marks them out from their peers. They are very likely to self-medicate to try to get some relief and to establish some control over their own function. Drugs, alcohol and other substances are commonly abused by young people living with stress disorders. Children may also become addicted to high stimulus activities such as computer games, dance, or sexual activity. What distinguishes these activities from equivalent activities in their peers is the joyless and obsessive way in which traumatised children attempt to lose themselves through external stimuli. Some criminal behaviour is also highly stimulating and may be attractive to hyperaroused children.

slide 9

Physical effects

- **Continued stress arousal may lead to:**
  - headaches
  - digestive disorders
  - respiratory disorders
  - other psychosomatic illnesses
  - muscle tension
  - aching joints
  - clumsiness
  - altered spatial awareness

Children living with stress injuries may experience a full range of psychosomatic conditions in addition to the somatisation of emotions already described. The impact on the body of perpetual stress arousal is immense, with the child being perpetually in survival mode. Some functions are exaggerated, such as pulse rate, breathing, blood pressure and muscle tension. Others such as digestion are suppressed. In the short term, the child may suffer day-to-day illnesses or disabling conditions such as headaches and aches and pains of the muscles or joints. In the long term, the immune system may become depleted, with increased risk of developing auto-immune disorders including disorders of thyroid function (see www.nyam.org/news/2003/030503.shtml, for example).

Emotional effects

- **Loss of ability to process experience through language**
- **Diminished or lost capacity for empathy**
- **Hypersensitivity to trauma in others**
- **Diminished range of emotions: terror or rage**
- **Loss of capacity for joy leads to diminished aesthetic and spiritual experience**
- **Feelings of worthlessness and shame**
- **Traumatic stress takes over core identity**

We are meaning-making animals, and without the ability to process our experience through language we cannot make sense of the world. Processing disorders lead to considerable disadvantages in learning. And children who find it difficult or impossible to put feelings into words are disadvantaged across the whole spectrum of school life, from informal social interaction to arenas of formal discussion and debate. They may be intellectually able, but their language will be lacking a discourse relating to their inner world, and every aspect of social and intellectual life is diminished as a result.

The capacity for empathy is also often affected by stress disorders after trauma. The preoccupation with trauma-related feelings and overwhelming unregulated stress gets in the way of ordinary sensitivity to others. On the other hand, traumatised children are often highly sensitive to the existence of stress disorders in others, and may gravitate towards others who have lived through trauma even though they are not aware of the history. This can lead to additional problems in the school setting, since hypersensitive children, who are easily triggered to panic or rage, can unintentionally multiply the stress reaction in each other.

The range of emotional reactions available to traumatised children is often reduced to the basic survival responses of terror and rage. These may be triggered by a wide variety of stimuli regarded by others as neutral. The child will be unlikely to recognise or reliably anticipate these responses, and will certainly not be able to control the automatic stress response even if they are cognitively aware that the response is irrational. Such children are at best uncomfortable companions and unpredictable class members, and at worst they may be dangerous to themselves or to others. If subject to such events, children urgently need informed help from those around them to regulate and manage their own physiological responses.

Real learning occurs when children are engaged with a subject and are finding it enjoyable and stimulating. Such learning engages children in experiences which are both aesthetic, involving the discernment of quality, and spiritual, connecting the child with the cosmos. Many traumatised children suffer anhedonia, the loss of the capacity to experience joy. With that loss, they also lose access to the delights of aesthetic and spiritual experience. For them the world has become barren and flat, a wasteland to be traversed but not appreciated. It becomes difficult for them to learn.

As we humans are creators of meaning, traumatised people will also try to make sense of their experience of the world. Since that experience is one of terror, pain, isolation and lack of pleasure, the child often concludes that they are worthless. This is a characteristic post-traumatic reaction. The damage to self-esteem may give rise to intense feelings of shame. This is bad news for adolescents in particular, who are acutely vulnerable to feeling shamed. Schools are settings in which children and young people have targets to reach in a highly competitive environment. Traumatised children are less likely to be able to reach the targets, and are more likely to find the shame of perceived failure overwhelming.

The process of creating meaning sits alongside the formation of identity. Our understanding of the world determines our sense of self. Children who have lived through the disintegration of traumatic stress will evolve a sense of self that is shaped by the traumatic events. We call this traumatic identity. It may mean that the child perceives their core identity as being a victim. Children and young people who think of themselves as doomed to suffer, or worthless, or deserving of punishment, or fatally attractive to abusers, or harbingers of destruction to others, or all of these, are unable to be happy or productive human beings.

If the child has been the victim of abuse they may also internalise the aggressor. This is a protective mechanism to allow the victim to acquire an identity after disintegration through identifying with the powerful abuser, and is well known in adult hostage situations as well as childhood abuse. In this case the traumatic identity may result in the child perpetrating harm against self or against others.

Social effects

- **Diminished impulse control may lead to social isolation or membership of deviant peer group**
- **Extreme reactions of terror or rage frighten others**
- **Diminished empathy limits social connectedness**
- **Being in survival mode restricts motivation to be sociable, except with other victims of trauma**
- **Avoidance restricts capacity to connect to others or to the sensory environment**
- **Diminished language functions restrict social accountability**
- **Taking on traumatic identity leads to persistent victim or aggressor behaviour**

The struggle to manage impulses they cannot account for leads many traumatised children to become socially isolated from their more socially accountable peers. Factors such as age, temperament and social circumstances will then lead them to be solitary, and often lonely, or to becoming members of a deviant peer group in which their difficulties are accepted and may indeed be promoted.

The diminished emotional range, and the extreme explosiveness of the emotional reactions, of traumatised children is scary to other people. Adults and other children react to the predictably unpredictable child with fear. This both isolates and frightens the traumatised child, and adds to the vicious spiral of terror which fuels the disorder. Information and understanding about the effects of trauma are vital for everybody around the recovering child. Only when people recognise and can account for their own fear in the presence of the child can they begin to manage themselves effectively and stop ascribing the bad feelings to the child who is the unwitting source of the disturbance.

Traumatic stress alters the capacity for empathy, changing the brain functions that allow us to be in touch with the experience of others. Children living with the various disorders that may follow unresolved trauma are therefore additionally hampered in their social relationships. Not only are they likely to provoke fear in others, but they are also unlikely to be able to make sense of the richer emotional world of most of their peers. The fear will reach them, other emotions are unlikely to be recognised.

Human beings are generally motivated to be sociable because it makes us feel good, it induces a sense of wellbeing and happiness to be part of a social group. Victims of trauma, however, have little access to sensations of wellbeing and contentment. This reduced motivation to sociability, alongside the experience of others as frightened and frightening, has serious implications for the intensely social life of the members of a school community. Most schools rely for their effective functioning on the inherent sociability of humans in groups. Traumatised children are likely to be critically unreliable in such settings. On the other hand, since humans do need social support, it is common for traumatised people to relate to each other rather than to the incomprehensible non-traumatised peer group. Children who have lived through trauma are sensitised to it, and tend to pick it up in others even when they have no knowledge of the personal history of the other. This can lead to difficulties for schools in trying to cope with groupings of children whose real, but usually unexpressed, mutual bond is the fact of having survived trauma. Such groups or groupings, bringing together the children who most struggle with making sense of the world and with regulating their own behaviour, can be sources of disorder in any school or community.

Children may also be disconnected from the day-to-day world of their own experience. Such radical disconnection cuts across the social life of any group. At home and at school the child will be difficult to live and work with if they lack or lose connectedness. We see children who do not know whether they are hot or cold, do not know if they feel hungry or thirsty, and do not know how to connect to events around them. Such disconnection also inhibits the already compromised ability to form sequential memories. It can be very difficult for traumatised children to carry a memory of the school day, so homework, news of forthcoming trips or other school events, and diary dates such as auditions, concerts or sports matches are all likely to be difficult to remember. The struggle to manage impulses they cannot account for leads many traumatised children to become socially isolated from their more socially accountable peers. Factors such as age, temperament and social circumstances will then lead them either to be solitary, and often lonely, or to becoming members of a deviant peer group in which their difficulties are accepted and may indeed be promoted.

Generally children of school age are expected to be socially accountable. They are able to give an account of themselves to others. Traumatised people, being locked in behaviours they cannot control, lose their accountability. This effect is more marked in childhood, since children are not as practised as adults at making themselves understood. When people are not accountable they tend to be shunned and excluded.

Traumatic stress causes the collapse of existing cognitive schemas, the core beliefs about ourselves and the world that shape our identity. Humans do not exist for long without a sense of identity, however, and new schemas form to fill the vacuum. These new core beliefs, such as 'bad things always happen to me', 'I am a dangerous person', 'anyone who loves me abuses me' and so on, create a new sense of identity which has been called traumatic identity. This will severely limit the possibilities open to the child. Some children take on a persistent victim identity. Others internalise the powerful aggressor, naturally enough since all children learn and grow by internalising the powerful adults in their lives; these children may then become aggressive or abusive towards others. And some children do both, and satisfy the harmful impulses of the internalised aggressor by harming the victim most close at hand, the self. All these behaviours in relation to traumatic identity are puzzling and frightening to others, and will have their effect on social life.

2

Lasting effects of maltreatment in infancy

- **When babies do not have their attachment needs met their development is affected**
- **Brain development is markedly different in maltreated babies**
- **This developmental impairment will be global in its effects**
- **Such impairment is in addition to any impairment resulting from genetic or pre-birth factors**

When babies are born their brains are very immature, more so than most mammals, and the brain will take years and not just days or weeks to reach its final form and structure. The effect of this is that humans are very intelligent, but also very vulnerable to adversity harming the developing brain. We now know that the infant brain is affected by a whole host of circumstances in the child's early life. These include genetic inheritance, temperament, pre-birth experience including maternal substance misuse and traumatic stress, and the experience of birth. We also know that, once the baby is born, the most significant single factor influencing the shape and structure of the developing brain is the quality of the adult response to the child's needs.

Babies are not able to regulate stress when they are first born. This ability will develop, or not, during the first eight months or so of life. They therefore depend on their caregivers to regulate stress for them, and babies encounter many stresses such as hunger, thirst, discomfort, pain, and fear. Since unregulated stress is very harmful to the developing child, they need to be able to control the reactions of the adults around them. To do this they produce attachment behaviours, activities that draw the attention and the remedial action of the caregiver. Such behaviours as crying, smiling, gurgling, waving, screaming, and so on are all attachment behaviours.

If the child gets what they need from the adults, then a pattern will develop in the brain that allows the child to begin to regulate stress for themselves. If not, then stress continues unregulated and the child develops a different brain. The differences will be both developmental, the brain growing differently in response to the maltreatment, and traumatic, the brain changing shape and structure as a result of injuries caused by unregulated stress.

The developmental impairment that results from unmet infant need is global in its effects. It is likely to leave the child with difficulties in two key activities of the brain: processing and regulating. These are fundamental functions, and the disorders that can result from maltreatment are predictably both persistent and extensive. Similar or related impairments may result from other factors affecting brain development, such as genetic predisposition and foetal injury, but these developmental disorders are additional. If the child has experienced multiple factors, the resulting disorders will occur together in complex ways, and make the work of helping the child to adapt to the impairments yet more challenging.

Brain development

- **The brain develops sequentially:**
  - Brain stem
    - state regulation: pre-birth – 8 months
  - Mid-brain
    - motor functioning: first year
  - Limbic brain
    - emotional functioning: 6 months–30 months
  - Cortex
    - cognitive functioning: 12 months–48 months

This developmental sequence refers to the formation of the structure of the brain. This takes place once the basic cells are laid down by about the middle of gestation, and continues throughout the first few years of life. In addition we are always, throughout our lives, making new connections within the brain, and these connections will in turn alter the structure. But the original shaping of the brain in infancy is not alterable, and takes place within certain critical periods of opportunity. Once those have passed, the person will have the basic structure that they will live with for the rest of their life. The function can be enhanced, but the basic structure cannot.

The brain stem controls such underlying states as waking and sleeping, breathing, and arousal and relaxation. If there are developmental impairments at this level of brain function, these states will be persistently dysregulated. That is, the organism will urgently, as a matter of survival, attempt to regulate but will fail, producing inconsistent consequences such as wakefulness, or sleepiness, or other maladaptive sleep patterns. Since the brain develops sequentially any brain stem impairment will also echo through the rest of the brain as it develops.

The parts of the brain that control motor function may also be affected by developmental impairment. Children with these difficulties may be poorly co-ordinated or clumsy, or they may struggle with spatial awareness and laterality, finding it difficult to distinguish left from right, and hence difficult to read or process sensory information about the world around them.

The limbic brain deals with feelings and impulses. Children whose caregivers are responsive and available enough to meet the child's needs are shaped in the period of limbic brain development by the many interactions that fill the world of the nurtured baby. Caregivers actively pattern the child to connect internal and external experience at this time, through responding in lively ways to the child's innate search for faces. The baby seeks out faces, and then sets up communication through eye contact, facial expressions and sounds. Responsive adults react to this, and begin to lead the baby in a complex dance of shared information. The effect of all this sociability on the developing brain produces reliable patterns for recognising feelings in self and others and recognising and managing impulses.

2

Thinking follows acting and feeling. The cortex is the last area of the brain structure to develop, and will function very differently depending on the shape and nature of the earlier formed brain structures. The host of cortical activities that we associate with being human – logical thought, music, art, poetry, mathematics, spirituality, and the establishment of complex social orders – all depend on the healthy development of much more primitive brain structures.

powerpoint
slide 14

Developmental impairment

- **Children may be stuck in age-inappropriate response patterns**
- **The resulting behaviours do not represent regression but are indicators that development has been impeded or distorted**

It is important to remember that we are dealing with injuries, which are never deterministic in the course of recovery. Each individual recovers differently. Each child reacts differently. What is being described is the increased probability that the child will be left with certain difficulties.

Examples of developmental impairment

- **Wetting and soiling**
- **Infantile fears**
- **Inability to distinguish:**
  - fact and fantasy
  - cause and effect
  - mine and yours
- **Lack of:**
  - empathy
  - emotional vocabulary
  - impulse regulation

Fearfulness after traumatic events, when children are programmed by harsh experience to expect the worst of the world, is different from being subject to infantile fears. Children who continue to experience the inchoate fears of babyhood will struggle to live alongside their peers who have long since moved on from such groundless terrors.

By the time they are at school, children are expected to be morally and ethically accountable human beings in an age-appropriate way. Children whose needs in relation to early attachment have not been met through deprivation or maltreatment often struggle both to process information (making sense of their own sensory experience) and to regulate their own function. Those whose early experience has not equipped them for the ordinary sociability of life will be ill-equipped to live alongside their more fortunate peers.

We tell children stories as a vital aspect of their learning and expect them to be able to make the distinction between story and life. If children cannot process information reliably, however, the ease with which the rest of us move between fact and fantasy in order to make sense of the world will confuse and puzzle them. And their own attempts to make use of counter-factual language will probably be seen as lying. Children with these developmental impairments are often described as compulsive liars because their attempts at conversation disturb others. We also need to be able to manage the counter-factual in order to understand negatives. Children who do not process negatives accurately may be seen as defiant when they are compliant, if the child hears "do not" as "do" then they will be constantly in trouble. And the future is always counter-factual. If we cannot distinguish between fact and fantasy we cannot plan our lives effectively.

Children who find it difficult to process information have no reliable sense of cause and effect. When children are looked after, they often catch up cognitively to the extent that they can distinguish more advanced logical patterns of cause and effect, but early maltreatment leaves them unable to make sense of what to others is simply basic and obvious. So a child may be able to do complex cognitive tasks at school, but fail to do simple cause and effect learning in relation to their behaviour. Or they

2

may be able to understand academic exercises, but be unable to generalise simple rules from instructions given. For example, 'Do not put the plug in the bath and leave the water running' is really about water rather than about baths and most young children would recognise that distinction and make the necessary generalisation. Yet an intelligent teenager two days later left the wash basin overflowing, and felt a deep sense of injustice at being expected to know that this would cause a problem.

We expect children, by the time they are at school, to be able to recognise boundaries of ownership and possession. This capacity to make distinctions and boundaries develops in early life and is adversely affected by maltreatment. Many looked after children struggle to understand the concept of mine and yours, and stealing is a common complaint of carers and school staff.

Empathy requires the ability to make sense of the messages transmitted by the behaviour of another person. Children who cannot easily process information cannot be empathic. The faces and the behaviour of others do not make sense. Traumatised children are also preoccupied and burdened, so have limited motivation to be in touch with the experience of others. Their own experience is exhausting enough.

Their own experience is also, however, mysterious. Information about their own inner state is just as difficult to process as information about the outside world. Children who have lived through significant adversity are likely to have a very impoverished emotional life. In particular, they often lack words for feelings, or if they have learned the words they do not accurately connect them to the inner states that others would recognise as emotions.

Managing our impulses is an essential element of our humanity. It requires both the ability to process information, to recognise that we are moved to do something, and the ability to regulate arousal, to exercise control over the impulse and make a decision about it. Children who live with developmental impairments are therefore likely to find it difficult to recognise or regulate impulses. This makes their behaviour both unpredictable and unaccountable.

Attachment and stress

- **Attachment behaviours are the infant response to stress**
- **Securely attached infants have emotionally available and responsive carers who enable the baby to regulate stress**
- **Insecurely attached infants do not develop stress regulation**

At birth babies do not have the ability to regulate stress. Arousal will be managed for them by their caregivers. As this attunement grows, the baby develops patterns in the brain for self-regulation. Healthy, well-treated babies sooner or later become able to regulate their own arousal. Those whose needs have not been met will adapt as best they can to living with unregulated stress.

Unmet attachment needs and stress injuries

- **When babies do not have their attachment needs met they suffer unregulated stress**
- **This overwhelming stress can lead to stress injuries**
- **These injuries can lead to additional developmental impairment**

The "double whammy" that affects many children whose early attachment needs have not been met is that failing to develop stress regulation leaves the baby with the problem of unregulated stress, which in turn causes injuries. The impairment of development may then be compounded by injuries that further limit the function of the developing brain.

2

The child's internal working model of the world: the STIRS model

- **When children are subject to developmental impairment they often have difficulty with:**
  - **S**tress
  - **T**rust and empathy
  - **I**mpulse
  - **R**age
  - **S**hame
- **Unmet attachment need STIRS up the child.**
- **The child STIRS up other people.**

Living and working with traumatised children is very challenging. It can be helpful to have working tools that add to a sense of structure. This mnemonic can help adults to recall the extreme difficulties faced by many children who live with developmental impairment.

Children who have difficulty with regulating stress may:

- **have disrupted sleep patterns**
- **be unable to tolerate excitement**
- **be very volatile**
- **be avoidant of a wide range of activities**
- **be withdrawn or spaced out**
- **be disconnected from their own experience**
- **cause others around them to feel tense and uncomfortable**

Stress dysregulation may lead to persistent hyperarousal or dissociation. It is important to recognise that children who dissociate are still suffering stress, and are being injured. The dissociation allows the child not to know that they are hurting, but it does not reduce the injury.

Children living with stress disorders find it as difficult to tolerate exciting events as they do to manage fear and anxiety. The physiology of stress disorder is so fragile that any disturbance of equilibrium is likely to produce distressed behaviour.

Children who have difficulty with trust may:

- show distrust, and trust nobody
- show mistrust, and trust the wrong people
- show indiscriminate trust, and be unable to distinguish between safe and unsafe people
- be more disturbing to live with the longer they are in placement because the lack of trust disrupts the core schemas of trustworthy carers

This use of language can help us to recognise the variety of difficulties that may arise over issues of trust. Like control, trust is a very primitive infantile response. It is as essential for the baby to trust caregivers as it is to control them, and the consequence of disruptions or distortions in the process of developing an appropriately trusting approach to others is an inability to perceive trustworthiness.

Since trust is also a primitive and fundamental issue for carers, disruptions of expectations can be very profound. We do expect that people we live with will trust us if we behave in a trustworthy way. If that does not happen, the impact on our own perception is destructive. And the effect here is cumulative. Many behavioural difficulties become easier with familiarity, but issues of trust have a reverse effect. The longer we live with someone who unjustly fails to trust us, the more our sense of reality and confidence in our own judgement slips. Carers need help to persist steadily with children who cannot offer trust.

Children who have difficulty with empathy may:

- be unable to form deep or lasting relationships
- be able to understand the thoughts but not the feelings of others, and be coldly manipulative
- be unable to make a reliable link between affect and emotion
- recognise affect and emotion in others but not in themselves
- hurt others without remorse
- cause others around them to feel disorientated and uncomfortable

The previous and following six slides are self-explanatory.

powerpoint slide 22

Children who have difficulty with regulating impulse may:

- be destructive of property
- constantly be in trouble with others
- be a danger to themselves or others
- be less and less socially acceptable as they get older
- be unable to account for their actions
- be vulnerable to being led or directed into antisocial behaviour

powerpoint slide 23

Children who have difficulty regulating rage may:

- be dangerous
- be unable to make or keep friends
- be a risk to others in social settings such as sports or any competitive environment
- be very destructive of property
- be terrified of their own dangerousness
- cause others around them to feel angry or frightened or both

powerpoint slide 24

Children who have difficulty managing shame may:

- be unable to accept responsibility for their own actions and mistakes
- become overwhelmed in competitive settings
- avoid shame through, for example, perfectionism or blame
- experience global instead of specific shame
- find making choices insupportable

powerpoint slide 25

Helpful areas of theory and research

- **Genetic inheritance and pre-birth experience**
- **Temperament**
- **Attachment theory and research**
- **Affect theory**
- **Trauma theory and research**
- **Resilience**
- **Planned environment therapy**
- **Family systems theory**

(Your local library will be able to help you find books and articles on these topics. Or you can use a search engine to find information on the internet. The list of useful books at the end of this pack will also give you some starting points for your own research.)

powerpoint slide 26

Making sense of life with maltreated children

- **Living with maltreated children changes the adults around the child**
- **Thoughts, feelings and beliefs are all affected**
- **Care-providing families and schools need help to find a way through the chaos that may come into their lives with the child**
- **Theory and research can provide maps to illuminate this new territory**

2

powerpoint slide 27

By making sense in this way

- **Carers and staff can be more patient – change is likely to be gradual and often imperceptible**
- **Carers and staff and their support networks can maintain their own health and resilience**
- **Everyone involved can introduce a discourse that involves helping the child to make sense of their own experience and to manage the things they find difficult**

powerpoint slide 28

To meet the needs of traumatised children we must:

- **understand the needs of the child**
- **recognise and develop the skills and resources of carers, and understand the factors that may adversely affect them**
- **accept the responsibilities of the social network to contain and support the recovering child and his or her carers**

Understanding the long-term effects of adversity in early childhood enables us to recognise and explain the special difficulties that many looked after children have with education. It becomes clear that after such adversity it can be very difficult for children to make sense of the world and to regulate their own responses to it. This makes it extremely difficult for them to manage in a complex and demanding environment like school. Yet this is not the end of the problem. For it is also observable that schools and carers often find looked after children particularly difficult to manage, over and above the overt problems the child brings with them. Again there is an additional factor that enters into the equation.

Why is it more difficult for schools to manage looked after children?

- **Issues over changes of placement**
- **Lack of adequate information**
- **Lack of clarity about roles and responsibilities**
- **Lack of knowledge and skill to deal with traumatised children**
- **Difficulty of containing post-traumatic behaviours in the school environment**
- **Effects of secondary traumatic stress**

This guide addresses specifically the difficulties that arise from the traumatic history of looked after children. Other resource and practice guides have addressed other issues. Some, as noted previously, have commented on the particular problems associated with post-traumatic behaviours:

> *The principal challenge in dealing with children in public care was identified as managing their challenging behaviour. There was good awareness that challenging behaviour arose from the young people's previous traumatic experiences ... School staff found it a challenge making allowances for unacceptable behaviour while giving the right messages to other pupils* (Fletcher-Campbell *et al*, 2003).

Strategies for creatively addressing and helping children to contain post-traumatic behaviours will be considered later. But first it is necessary to consider the dynamics of working with trauma that can block creativity. The idea of secondary traumatic stress will provide a model for exploring these processes.

SECTION 2
The adults

2

Trauma is catching: secondary traumatic stress in child care

- **Secondary traumatic stress is the stress that results from caring for or about someone who has been traumatised**
- **It can result in injuries similar to those produced by primary trauma**
- **People who are empathic, and/or have experienced trauma in their own lives, and/or have unresolved personal trauma are vulnerable**
- **People who care for traumatised children are particularly vulnerable to secondary traumatic stress**

Living and working with traumatised children changes us over and above the ordinary processes of ageing. Some of the changes are undoubtedly to our benefit. Children who have survived adversity are interesting and courageous people who can teach us a great deal about ourselves and others and constantly provoke us to stretch ourselves and become more creative and flexible. They also provoke other reactions, however, that can be much less good for our health.

The knowledge base about secondary traumatic stress is now considerable (see, for example, the extensive work of Charles Figley on this subject). People who care for and work with victims of trauma can develop symptoms of post-traumatic disorders as though they themselves had been traumatised. All the adults around the traumatised child are vulnerable to developing these symptoms. Other children who care for or about the traumatised child are also vulnerable.

The good news is that secondary traumatic stress is both preventable and, if it does occur, manageable and treatable. And the first step to containing and managing secondary trauma is knowledge.

Most clinicians make a distinction between secondary traumatic stress and burnout. Both are stress disorders, and for the individual will have an impact on effective functioning, but there are differences in how the conditions are generated, and therefore differences in how they can be effectively treated. It is likely that many people involved in working with children may at different times, or indeed at the same time, suffer both.

Broadly speaking, burnout is employment or role-related, has gradual onset, and is linked to negative factors in the work environment such as lack or loss of support. Burnout can usually be resolved by work-related interventions. The individual is likely to be changed in relation to work, but core identity generally remains intact. Most people who are suffering burnout are aware that they are affected and can accurately ascribe the causes of their disorder.

Secondary traumatic stress is specific to working with a particular child, and is likely to be of rapid or sudden onset. This onset may occur in people who have worked with many similarly traumatised children; there seems to be a critical point at which defences collapse. If secondary traumatic stress is not resolved it may lead on to disorders similar to primary traumatic stress disorders. These are global disorders that affect every aspect of the personal functioning of the individual concerned. People affected lose contact with their own experience, so are likely to be unaware of the developing disorder.

2

2

Signs and indicators

- **Distressing emotions**
  - anger, tearfulness, fearfulness
- **Unexplained changes in health**
  - sleep, eating, physical illnesses
- **Physiological arousal**
  - jumpiness, nightmares, hypervigilance
- **Avoidance of working with traumatic material**

Change in existing patterns is the key to recognising these signs and indicators. If someone is characteristically bad tempered, then anger is not an indicator. But patient people who become inexplicably irritable and angry may be developing symptoms.

Patterns are important. One indicator on its own means nothing, but a pattern of several changes should sound an alarm.

It is vital to be knowledgeably self-aware, but this will fail in severe cases. It is therefore also vital to have others who understand the condition and will tell us if we are changing. We must also commit ourselves to hear and act on such information even though it feels inaccurate because of the changes in our functioning. We can similarly act as monitors for the wellbeing of others.

The indicators listed are in increasing order of concern. Most people who work with children will sometimes experience distressing emotions. It is more worrying if physical health problems develop. It is more worrying still if profound psychological changes occur. It is most worrying if the person becomes avoidant, since at that stage the condition will, without strong intervention, become self-perpetuating. All these worries can be resolved by programmes of prevention and treatment.

Avoidance is a difficult concept for us to hold on to. It is a mechanism that protects us from becoming overwhelmed in situations of danger. Faced with threat, the mind closes down consciousness of the stimulus that will disturb us and diverts our attention elsewhere. It is then impossible for us to notice the trigger stimulus and it is also impossible for us to notice that we are avoidant. This double concealment is necessary if the defence is to work. If we were able to think about the fact that we are avoidant, we would already have brought the existence of the threat into our consciousness.

The only protection, and the only treatment, for avoidance behaviour is the help we receive from other people. There are obvious limits to this. One is that the greater the threat to our equilibrium the greater our resistance to hearing from our kind friends or colleagues that we are avoidant. We are also less able to seek or to understand such information as we become more disordered. And if the threat is a shared one, if many in the network are troubled by contact with the traumatised child, then there will be a shared avoidance that will be immensely powerful. We have to work very hard at staying open to preventing and stopping avoidance.

powerpoint
slide 32

Signs of developing disorder

● **Impairment of day-to-day functioning, leading to such changes in behaviour as:**
  - missed or cancelled appointments
  - decreased use of support networks
  - chronic lateness
  - poor self-care
  - increased feelings of isolation, alienation and lack of appreciation

In mixed training groups this slide gives rise to some wry amusement, as each occupational group is likely to be able to recognise one of the other groups in the description. It is always easier to see developing disorder in others than in ourselves.

It is essential to recognise that stress disorders make us less able to use support. This fundamental irony is the cause of many serious problems in the world of child care.

2

Impact of STSD on individuals

● **Performance**
  - decrease in quality and quantity
  - increased mistakes
  - avoidance of tasks
  - perfectionism
  - obsessiveness
  - exhaustion
  - irresponsibility

● **Morale**
  - decrease in confidence
  - apathy
  - dissatisfaction
  - negativity
  - feel incomplete
  - subsume own needs
  - detachment

Secondary traumatic stress is disintegrative. It destroys core aspects of the self, including those structures of belief about ourselves and the world that shape all our attitudes and behaviour. Simultaneously we become less effective and less able to feel effective.

It is instructive to ask occupational groups suffering any symptoms of disorder to reflect on themselves as they were in the past. As they think about the person they were when they were chosen to do the work they have undertaken, they can remember that they were perceived by competent others as skilled and able. This reflection often produces changes in thinking about secondary trauma, as people become aware that they still are that person, and can recover all that sense of self worth and potency. It is also an indicator to them of the journey they have been taking, and the possible harmful consequences if they do not give themselves some care.

Impact on whole network

- **Withdrawal**
- **Lack of appreciation**
- **Impatience**
- **Increase in conflict**
- **Poor communication**
- **Persecutor/victim/rescuer dynamic**

If the network around the child is disordered it begins to show in the behaviour of all concerned. People whose work involves a wide range of people skills become much less able to work with one another. They tend to withdraw into their professional silos, as the current jargon has it. Perhaps such behaviour should be taken as symptomatic, an indicator of disorder needing therapeutic attention, rather than being made the subject of professional targets.

A perceptive comment from the children of carers was that they could tell when things were going badly for the foster child because the social worker stopped seeing the family with gratitude. Indeed, the children felt the social worker at that point stopped seeing the family as anything except a problem. As the young people said, 'We're the same family. We haven't changed. We haven't suddenly become a problem family. All the problems came with fostering. But now we never even hear a thank you.' Such loss of a sense of appreciation of the others in the child's network, with all their strengths and weaknesses, is commonplace in the presence of developing disorder.

Traumatised children sometimes seem to move within a small personal cloud of war. Wherever they go there are people who fall out with one another. This is characteristic of the effects of secondary traumatisation. Overt and covert conflicts between the people around the child are another indicator that secondary traumatic stress may be affecting the network. Again, guided reflection can be illuminating. People can consider the relationships they have with the adult networks around other children. It is likely they will find that the most conflictual relationships are those associated with traumatised children. Often when reflecting in this way, people recognise that this effect goes beyond the fact that the child may be presenting challenging behaviour. It extends to interpersonal conflicts that are inexplicable without some model for understanding how we are changed.

People who work with traumatised children are professional communicators. It is therefore striking how depleted they can become in their communication with each other. It is further evidence of alteration in functioning in relation to the work with the child.

Finally, mature and otherwise emotionally intelligent people can find themselves locked in the dynamics of oppression. All the roles that may be enacted in the richness and subtlety of human relationships are then reduced to the three oppressive roles of victim, persecutor and rescuer. Every possible relationship within the network may become enmeshed in this perverse dynamic, with each participant assigning a different role to the others. The only movement at this stage is within this oppressive triangle, and it requires a strong intervention to release the network into a more graceful way of being.

2

Vulnerability and resilience in adults and children

- **Adversity may lead to recovery or disorder**
- **Dynamic factors affect the probable outcome**
  - Individual factors and social factors
  - Physical, psychological and spiritual factors
- **People are always both vulnerable and resilient**

All human beings are resilient, and all are vulnerable. This is the common humanity that links us to the children entrusted to our care.

Trauma means "injury". Traumatic stress is simply that level of stress that injures us. The outcome of every injury is complex and cannot be deterministic. We respond differently to different injuries, and we respond differently to the same injury on different days or at different times of our lives.

Traumatic stress is a condition that involves both external events and internal responses. There has to be something real going on in our environment, and we have to perceive it as horrifying. Not surprisingly, therefore, the factors that protect us and enable us to recover are also both personal and social. Individual factors include genetic inheritance, temperament, prior mental health, physical health, linguistic ability, a strong and adaptable moral code, spirituality, and creativity. Social factors include strong but flexible networks, close confiding relationships, contact with people who understand trauma, and supportive supervision at work.

Taking care of the caretakers

- **People working with traumatised children may develop secondary traumatisation and become less effective individually and collectively**
- **It will be impossible to meet the needs of the children if the adults cannot work together effectively**
- **It is therefore vital to give attention to the whole network responsible for the care and education of the child**
- **Only then can the needs of the children be given proper attention**

SECTION 3
What you can do

powerpoint
slide 37

What do children need?

- **Recognition**
- **Help with attachment**
  - Affective attunement: soothing/stimulation/trust
  - Reintegrative shame: impulse/choice/responsibility
  - Sociability: self-control/reflection/reciprocity
- **Appropriate treatment for trauma:**
  - Stabilisation: safety/explanation/words for feelings
  - Integration: physiological/emotional/cognitive
  - Adaptation: social connectedness/self-esteem/joy

There is growing consensus about the steps needed to promote recovery after trauma. Generally clinicians recognise the complex and chaotic nature of the disorders, and advocate a phased approach to recovery. This approach establishes a first phase of connecting, a second phase of processing, and a third phase of adapting socially after the personal transformation of trauma. Each of these phases can be seen as having three component parts. This leads to a nine-point curriculum for supporting recovery. This should not, however, be seen as anything more than an outline, with suggestions to engender the creativity of those who care for the child.

Children who have been maltreated in infancy will also need to recover from any developmental impairments. This process also lends itself to the same structure, with the same proviso about the absolute need to learn each child and to recognise that each unique person will need us to start afresh with our own creativity.

Although the process of recovery goes in phases, it should be recognised that children do not follow a neat course through recovery. They circle back, revisit earlier stages on the journey, and also at times move ahead, testing out activities and processes that will not be fully efficacious for them until later in their recovery. It is essential that treatment for trauma allows this freedom for the child to move through the recovery journey in their own time and at their own pace.

The earlier the maltreatment or trauma, the longer it may take to recover from it. For some children the process may take much of a lifetime.

Whatever is good for children as they recover is also good for the network around the child as they prevent or treat secondary trauma.

2

powerpoint
slide 38

A nine-point curriculum for working effectively with traumatised children

1 **Safety first: soothing hyperaroused children**
2 **Engaging: stimulating interest and teaching about trauma**
3 **Trusting and feeling: learning connectedness**
4 **Managing the self: regulating impulse and regulating the body**
5 **Managing feelings: choices and emotional processing**
6 **Taking responsibility: making sense of the world we share**
7 **Developing social awareness: learning self-control**
8 **Developing reflectivity: promoting self-esteem**
9 **Developing reciprocity: learning that life can be joyful**

Living and working effectively with traumatised children is often counter-intuitive. It has to be learned. That is the bad news. The good news is that an approach that works with traumatised children will work with *all* children.

The argument is often made that it is not possible to run a whole school, or family, or establishment, for the benefit of the minority. As the DfES research showed (Fletcher-Campbell *et al*, 2003), it is a real concern of teachers that, if they meet the challenges set by the post-traumatic behaviour of looked after children, they may do a disservice to all the other children in the school. This recognises appropriately that traumatised children have special needs, but demonstrates that the counter-intuitive nature of dealing with trauma leads to an unnecessary limitation of responses.

The apparent choice is between meeting the needs of the majority and risking the social exclusion of looked after children, or meeting the needs of looked after children and letting down the majority. But this apparent choice is a false dichotomy. The real choice is this: we can establish an environment and a way of working that will be effective for non-traumatised children but will tend to exclude traumatised children, or we can establish an environment and a way of working that will be effective for *all* children.

Children who live with developmental and functional impairments do have special needs. Traumatised children need clear structures and firm boundaries, they need safety and security, they need to be enabled and encouraged to learn, and they need all this to be sturdy enough to withstand the chaos of disorder. They also need the people around them to be very resilient, so that they too can survive the chaos of the world of the child. Put like that, however, it is clear that meeting these needs would provide very well for children who have not had to live through this level of adversity.

The nine-point structure here proposed offers a way of planning an environment and approach that will work. It can also be adapted and used to provide a structure for managing particular incidents of post-traumatic behaviour. It is drawn from robust research and theory on attachment, trauma and resilience.

The nine steps are progressive, drawn from the successive phases of treatment for post-traumatic disorders. As with those phases, however, the process is not linear. We will always be trying activities and interventions from later stages to see if they are useful, and if the child may be ready for them. And children will constantly cycle back to earlier steps to consolidate progress and to gain reassurance and stability at times of stress. The progression is therefore not a template, but is more of an organic matrix that gives us a way of understanding why children struggle more with some things than others, and why they struggle more at some times than others.

It is pointless to expect a child who is hyperaroused to be engaged with emotional processing, which comes much later in the progression. And a child who last week was fully engaged with therapy but who has cycled back to hyperarousal will now not be able to manage emotional processing. Similarly children who are dissociated will not be accessible to practice regulating impulse. First they must get connected with their own experience, then they can begin to work out what bits of their experience precede impulsive behaviour. So the process is developmental and practical, as befits a structure designed to address developmental and functional impairments.

2

Safety first: soothing hyperaroused children

- **Attachment-related ideas**
  - Provide and sustain a relaxing environment
  - Ensure that adults set the emotional tone
  - Encourage and enable the child to turn to the carers for soothing
  - Bring relaxation into the awareness of the child and encourage practice
  - Discourage dependence on high stimulus activities

- **Trauma-related ideas**
  - Stay aware of the terror
  - Think first of the physical environment: lowest level interventions
  - Five senses tour of the environment
  - Create safe spaces at home and at school
  - Use self appropriately to deal with a terrified flight animal: voice, gestures, expression
  - Use groupwork skills to create sense of safety

Most school-age children can regulate arousal most of the time. They do not usually find their environment over-stimulating. Traumatised children, by contrast, are likely to struggle to regulate arousal at all. Their interface with the environment is the physiological equivalent of a physical raw wound.

A physically relaxing and calming environment is good for everyone. Adults must take responsibility for ensuring that any setting that may include traumatised children is designed to be a calm and peaceful space.

Reflecting on the space, either actually or in the imagination, it is useful to visit every area using all five senses. What does the space look like? What is the quality of light? Colours? Shapes? Textures? What is the ambient sound? How does it smell? What is the distance between people? Research indicates that all these factors influence human physiology at an unconscious level. This is not a matter of aesthetics, which have to do with joy, but is to do with much more primitive state responses of arousal and relaxation. It is also instructive to complete the five senses tour of the environment as though with the senses of the child. Apart from obvious differences of height and understanding, the critical difference for the child may arise from disorders of processing. The child may inhabit a vastly different sensory world. Great learning can come from trying to get inside that sensory experience.

Hyperaroused children exert a powerful influence on the emotional tone wherever they are. It is important that the adults stay aware of the power of the excitement and stay in control of the emotional tone of the environment.

The provision of a safe space agreed with the child will greatly help the incidence of hyperaroused behaviours. It acknowledges that the child has a real and explicable difficulty and honours their struggle to contain and manage the stress. It will also help and encourage the child to begin to notice the first signs of arousal and take preventive action, which is the beginning of self-management.

Traumatised children will crave high stimulus activities. They are addicted to their own stress hormones. Sometimes people think that it is right to allow children to choose every aspect of their own life, and children spend their whole time buzzing. This is bad for their health. They do experience serious discomfort in low stimulus environments. We need to help them live with and through this discomfort. They will call it boredom, but it will have a different, much more intense, quality from the mild ennui that most children would experience if unoccupied.

Adults need to practise 'not startling the horses' when working with traumatised children, for children, like horses, are flight animals. Unfortunately many hyperaroused children appear anything but timid, and this leads people to treat them as frightening rather than frightened. The counter-intuitive technique is to assume with any challenging child that fear is a large part of the equation for the child, and at the same time to recognise that this will engender fear in the adult. So we must contain and manage our own fear, and soothe the terror of the child.

Frightened children spread hyperarousal throughout the groups of which they are part. This can be a recipe for disaster, but is also an opportunity. It can be very effective to intervene indirectly through helping some other member of the group to contain or divert the arousal.

Engaging: stimulating interest and teaching about trauma

- **Attachment-related ideas**
  - Provide appropriate environmental stimulation for adults and children
  - Use storytelling and activities requiring use of the imagination
  - Encourage expression of experience and development of emotional intelligence
  - Bring dissociation into awareness, develop sense of protector self and observer self

- **Trauma-related ideas**
  - Learning about the effects of trauma is part of the treatment
  - Everyone around the child can contribute to this learning
  - Each child needs us to learn how to teach them what they need to know
  - Stories and metaphors are powerful tools for teaching about overwhelming events

Children can make no progress while they remain closed off from their own experience. We need to provide environments which are calming to soothe hyperarousal, but which are also stimulating, to engage the child with their own sensory experience. The five senses tour is again useful, this time examining the space for the effect it may have in enabling and provoking the dissociated child to connect with their own senses.

Once the child is making some connection, it is important to translate the experience into words so that it is processed and locked into memory. This will then enable the child to begin to use imagination, which is a further extension of connectedness to their inner world.

Learning about trauma is a vital stage of recovery. Children who are living with developmental impairments and post-traumatic disorders are usually terrified of their own unpredictability and unaccountability. Learning about trauma helps. It also reconnects the child to the rest of humanity. Disorder after trauma is predictable, even if the resulting behaviours are not. Children can learn that all humans are vulnerable, and that they have been injured. If whole groups of children learn about trauma, they all benefit. For those who have not yet suffered any significant harm, prior learning enhances their resilience and helps them to understand their less fortunate peers.

Many great stories speak the truths of trauma. If the wall of dissociation can be broken down, children will then start seizing these metaphors and making them their own.

Dissociation is a benign human capacity. We need to be able to split our experience. Children who dissociate as a result of disorder need help to understand the benefits of bringing the process into awareness and using it constructively. They can be encouraged to reflect on times when switching off has helped them – at the dentist's, for example – and then honour their protector self that keeps them safe. Then they can think about the self that allows them to think about bits of themselves, and recognise that they have an inner observer self who is very important to them. The existence in awareness of an observer is a protector against disorder.

Trusting and feeling: learning connectedness

- **Attachment-related ideas**
  - Encourage open discussion of issues of trust
  - Distinguish between distrust and mistrust
  - Accept the level of trust the child has to offer
  - Recognise the effect on trustworthy people of not being trusted
  - Deal with lying and stealing as issues of trust – relationship not punishment

- **Trauma-related ideas**
  - Encourage the child to express inner states in words, even though they will find this difficult
  - Be clear and expressive about our own feelings
  - Notice the non-verbal signals of feelings and help the child to recognise and name what is happening
  - Identify self-transcending as well as self-assertive emotions

Trust cannot be forced. The most important issue in relation to the child trusting us is to expect nothing and be delighted with anything. This will help mitigate the harmful effects of not being trusted. Developmentally impaired children need to learn to value trust. Every occasion of untrustworthiness should be treated first as an issue of trust and only secondarily as the behaviour in itself.

Until children can begin to express feelings in words they cannot process emotions. If children have no access to language, they will need us to discover some other means to symbolise their inner experience in order for them to process it. That is the way we work.

Using language with children who live with developmental impairments is a tricky matter. Processing disorders make it likely that what the child hears will rarely be what the adult says. It is vital to recognise this, and to keep checking back that what we think we said is what the child thinks they heard.

Children living with developmental and functional impairments need to be constantly exposed to models of emotional intelligence. The adults around the child need to be willing to be appropriately emotionally expressive, offering clear statements about their own inner world to help the child to see how it is to be in touch with the flux and flow of emotional experience. Such statements must of course be about the experience and not about the child. 'I feel worried' is a different statement from 'You are worrying me', and a more honest one at that. If we own our feelings, we are also containing them, which the child will appreciate.

Salespersons and hypnotists learn to recognise very subtle physiological signals – so must the adults responsible for traumatised children. When we observe changes, we can tell the child and see if we can help them to put a feeling word to the physiological change. As trust develops, some children will then do this in reverse, which is also part of the learning: 'Why have you gone red?' 'Because I'm embarrassed' 'Why are you crying?' 'Because I feel sad' and so on.

It is easy to see self-assertive emotions. These are the strong mammal reactions of the nervous system, such as rage and fear. It is more demanding to notice the parasympathetic emotions such as compassion, awe and joy. It can be particularly difficult to notice these occurring in traumatised children whose emotional range is so limited. Yet self-transcending emotions are vital to our humanity. It is well worth the effort to notice their occurrence and to make the comment that draws the emotion to the attention of the child.

2

Managing the self: regulating impulse and regulating the body

● **Attachment-related ideas**
  ● Avoid asking 'why did you do that?'
  ● Instead invite reflection linking inner state with actions
  ● Encourage the child to be interested in their own inner state with regard to their behaviour
  ● Notice and comment on small indicators of self-regulation
  ● Encourage children to build on growing capacity for self-management
● **Trauma-related ideas**
  ● Learn the child – what helps this child to relax?
  ● Discuss relaxation and soothing activities with the child
  ● Encourage the child to practise a range of approaches to changing their own physiology
  ● Demonstrate willingness to practise new techniques to manage stress

Children of school age are expected to be morally accountable. Developmentally impaired children are not. The development in the first and second years of life of impulse regulation provides the template in the second and third years for being able to think about our actions. 'Why did you do that?' is a silly question at six months of age, and a meaningless one at 18 months. But by the age of three, most children will try to answer it and make a reasonable attempt to describe their inner state. Maltreatment in the formative period reduces or prevents such accountability. Later trauma will also block access to inner experience, so that children who were previously morally accountable may lose that capacity when traumatised.

The consequence of disorder is dysregulation. That is, the child as an organism will be attempting and failing to self-regulate. This pre-conscious activity produces a persistent sense of failure even when the child is doing nothing. This becomes much worse when the child is challenged to account for their actions and cannot do so. They have then failed to do something they were asked to do, and they have also failed to do something that manifestly is easy for their peers. These failures distress them.

The child needs us to help them notice and accept that this accountability is more difficult for them than it is for other people, and then to reflect on the links between their inner state and their actions. 'What happens inside you just before you ... fly into a rage ... hit people ... cut yourself ...?' are more interesting and productive questions than 'Why did you do it?'. The answers to such questions are always nonsense, but they are important nonsense. They are genuine information about the inner world of this child. One eight-year-old said, of his previously unaccountable and uncontrollable rages, 'I get hot in my chest, then I start to breathe like this (panting) and I see colours'. A 15-year-old, assessed as dangerous said, also describing uncontrolled rage, 'There's a buzzing in my head here (just behind the left ear), and then I get small and the other person gets very big'. Both these children went on to gain management of the rage.

Once the child is able to say something, and anything will do, about their inner state, they can be helped to gain some control. The key is to stay very close to the experience of the child and to work with them creatively and experimentally. Encourage them to try different ways of gaining some physiological self-management and to report on progress, since putting inner experience into words is one object of the exercise. The eight-year-old above was clearly identifying breathing changes as an indicator. Breathing exercises helped him to take conscious control of the unconscious process. And working with his own response taught him to respect and value the trustworthiness of his own body to give him messages and keep him safe.

Children need to see that adults around them are willing to try new techniques in stress management and willing to talk about the experience.

powerpoint slide 43

Managing feelings: choices and emotional processing

- **Attachment-related ideas**
  - If children struggle with choice, openly discuss limiting their choices in order to help them learn
  - Restrict choice-making to social situations that are least stressful
  - Encourage child to recognise and celebrate choices successfully made
  - Encourage child to recognise and celebrate learning from mistakes

- **Trauma-related ideas**
  - Help child to engage with therapy if available and appropriate
  - Encourage child to feel more in control – space, time, activities
  - Expect and contain disturbed behaviour
  - Manage contact with disturbing people and places
  - Ensure carers are supervised

Shame is the issue here. The affect of shame is a protective inhibitor of impulse in babies and toddlers. It allows the child who has not yet developed the capacity to assess risk and who is becoming able to act on impulses to live safely in a dangerous world. The securely attached infant will check with their attuned caregiver before acting. If the carer approves, the child feels pleasure. If the carer reacts adversely, the child feels shame. In secure relationships, such shame is transient and essential to protect the child from harm. The child quickly reintegrates with the carer and experiences the pleasure of renewed attunement. That child has a pre-verbal pattern for making mistakes, learning from them and saying sorry.

In maltreated children this process goes awry. Then the child grows to experience shame as another overwhelming stress. They dysregulate to shame. Such children cannot learn from their mistakes and they cannot apologise. Once in a hole, they just tend to keep digging.

If shame is overwhelming then choice tends to be impossible. Every time we make a choice we risk making the wrong choice, which, if you are hypersensitive to shame, is the same as making a mistake.

First the child needs us to recognise and acknowledge that they find making choices more difficult than other people. Then they need us to help them manage shame, which begins with managing the physiology of overwhelm. And finally they need us to help them manage choice-making. This may sometimes mean limiting and rehearsing choices, especially in the sort of social situation where they would feel particularly exposed to shame. Trips and outings, being very public, are difficult occasions and traumatised children may suffer agonies if asked to make simple choices about, for example, menus or drinks in such exposed settings. Limiting the choices, or discussing them beforehand with the child, can make a great difference to having a calm and enjoyable day out.

The growing capacity to connect with their own emotional experience may mean that the child will need and be ready for therapy. If so, they will also need substantial social support, and so will their carers, who will bear the brunt of disturbed behaviour.

Taking responsibility: making sense of the world we share

- **Attachment-related ideas**
  - Allow child to let go of excessive or inappropriate responsibilities
  - Encourage child to allow adults to be in control appropriately
  - Give clear messages about taking responsibility for our own behaviour
  - Celebrate any evidence of the child taking appropriate responsibility for behaviour

- **Trauma-related ideas**
  - Recognise the power of traumatic identity
  - Expect the child to resist redefining their own identity
  - Provide the child with choices about how they see themselves
  - Emphasise the benefits of positive self-image
  - Model giving and receiving compliments

Maltreated children are often burdened children. They carry huge and inappropriate responsibilities. They may be the caretaker for their own parents or family members, or they may believe that they are responsible for the abuse they suffered, or they may be stuck at the toddler stage of magical thinking and believe that they are responsible for holding the universe together. At the same time they are functionally unable to take responsibility for their own actions. They are morally unaccountable. This is a toxic mixture, and the child will need sensitive help to let go of one set of responsibilities and assume the responsibilities that properly belong to them.

Even when the child has developed the capacity to recognise and process their own emotions, and even if they have been engaged with therapy, the traumatised child will still be left with cognitive schemas that are trauma-based. The belief systems and deep cognitive structures of traumatised people are distorted by trauma. In particular the three core assumptions of healthy humans identified by Janoff-Bulman (1992) – that the world is benevolent, that the world is meaningful, and that the self is worthy – are shattered by trauma.

Children who believe that the world is terrifying, chaotic and meaningless and that they are evil and unlovable, are not going to have happy lives. Yet these cognitive constructs are so deep that they affect the very identity of the child. These are core beliefs about the self and the world. Humans resist having their identity redefined, and that is equally true when the identity is itself harmful and destructive. Adults need to remember that this resistance to developing a more benign identity is inevitable and is based on protective mechanisms. We have to allow the child to let go gradually of their traumatic identity and replace it with the image of self we are patiently reflecting to them through our positive regard.

Developing social awareness: learning self-control

- **Attachment-related ideas**
  - Encourage discussion about self and others in social situations
  - Identify and rehearse social situations requiring self-control in the child
  - Encourage creative problem-solving towards such situations
  - Promote activities motivating social accountability such as sport, drama, music

- **Trauma-related ideas**
  - Encourage friendships and social interaction
  - Reflect with the child on issues of friendship and sociability
  - Provide and encourage outings and adventures
  - Encourage the child to broaden the range of their social connections and to be interested in people generally

Once the child is beginning to develop the capacity for personal responsibility and positive cognitive structures, they can turn their attention outward and discover the world of social interaction. This will be very scary. Traumatised children, as we have seen, will still have a very tenuous grasp on self-regulation, and may have a very different sensory experience of the world from other children. Processing disorders and regulatory disorders make children very fragile in social settings.

The child may now be ready for formal as well as informal bits of social learning. Problem-solving techniques, conflict resolution, anti-bullying strategies and so on are worth trying, although they may engender panic and overwhelm if the child is not yet ready. In which case, they need to cycle back to practising physiological self-regulation. These impairments are very persistent. Everyone, including the child, will need to be very patient and to notice and comment on every tiny sign of progress.

powerpoint slide 46

2

Developing reflectivity: promoting self-esteem

- **Attachment-related ideas**
  - Promote the use of feedback as a general feature of life for children and adults
  - Encourage the use of tools for reflection such as keeping a diary
  - Help children deal with feedback from a range of social situations
  - Be creative about ways to help the child become fearlessly reflective

- **Trauma-related ideas**
  - Encourage the child to take over responsibility for their own space and to make it beautiful
  - Now the child will be ready to hear praise and appreciation, which should be freely offered – catch them doing something good
  - Provide and comment on role models of centred people who are comfortable in their own life

Where shame is an issue, children will struggle with feedback, yet without it they cannot learn. So feedback needs to be an ordinary feature of life for everyone around the child, enabling them to feel safe with it. As ever, we need to make the child aware of the difficulty so that we can openly help them develop strategies and techniques to manage feedback. They need to be aware that not everyone feels so overwhelmed by constructive criticism and praise, and that it is the overwhelm and not the feedback that is the problem.

Self-esteem work is often done with children too early in their recovery. Not that we would ever not be doing work on self-esteem, of course, but we should expect that in the early stages of recovery the response to such work may be adverse. The early stages of recovery should not last more than twenty years, and may be much less.

Developing reciprocity: learning that life can be joyful

- **Attachment-related ideas**
  - Share thoughts and feelings
  - Apologise when we hurt the child
  - Encourage the child to reflect on our experience as well as their own
  - Invite the child to take our position – ' What do you think I should do about this?' in response to child's behaviour
  - Accept that we are a problem for the child

- **Trauma-related ideas**
  - Provide a wide range of aesthetic experiences – books, poetry, music, art, drama, dance, cookery, crafts, interior decoration, and so on
  - Encourage talk about joyful experience
  - Record happiness – journals, photographs, pictures, poems, memorabilia
  - Encourage reminiscence about joyful experiences

At last children will, if all goes well, become personally, morally and socially accountable human beings. Then they can enter into genuine reciprocal relationships, and if, through all the storms and difficulties we have stayed steady for them, we may benefit from their company.

Yet we will still be a problem to the child. It is usual for adults to think of the traumatised child as a problem. This can prevent us from seeing how much of a problem we are to the child. They need to relate to us, yet we are mysterious and inexplicable. We constantly set them challenges that cut across their deepest understandings of the world. We respond to them in ways they find unpredictable and frightening. We are their problem.

Throughout their time with us, they will be working hard to solve the problem we are to them. We owe it to them to work as hard at solving the problem they are to us. And we also owe it to them to make ourselves as transparent as possible, to help them to understand us.

Traumatised children usually suffer anhedonia, the loss of the capacity to experience joy. Even when they do begin to find genuine pleasure in life, they are often unable to process it, so that it is transient and unmemorable. It is very important for the recovering child to have experiences of joy and to learn to commit these to memory through language. They need us to help them become joyful people.

Applying the nine-step structure to dealing with individual incidents of post-traumatic behaviour

1 Safety first

Before all else remember the terror of children living with disorder. take steps to bring down the arousal. If possible, move away from the location where the event was triggered. Try to be in a space the child regards as safe. Have an identified person who is seen by the child as safe to deal with the incident. If possible have two people, one to support the child and provide safety and one to manage the process of discipline.

2 Engaging

The child will not hear you, or will not process what is said, while hyperaroused. If necessary, provide an immediate but temporary response to manage the situation. Then agree to wait until later, perhaps even the next day, when the child is less stressed, to take the disciplinary process forwards.

3 Trusting and feeling

When the child is able to hear and to process what they have heard, ensure that their attention is engaged. Establish your trustworthiness and that you are not going to harm the child. Comment on their obvious strong feelings and offer them a narrative that starts from feelings.

4 Managing the self

Ask the child to reflect on the inner state experiences that went with the incident. Invite calm reflection on and interest in the answers. Even if the answer is 'don't know', that is an interesting piece of information about this child's inner world.

5   Managing feelings

Acknowledge that shame is uncomfortable and for this child can be overwhelming. Help the child to think of ways to prevent feeling overwhelmed and to manage shame. Clarify that the child always has choices, and explore how making choices may be more difficult for the child than for other people.

6   Taking responsibility

Now provide a narrative for what happened. Be clear about what you know and what is hearsay. Check that the child has heard and understood. Take responsibility for the narrative, listen to what the child has to say and amend the narrative if necessary. Then give a clear statement of the consequences. Reassure the child that living with the consequences of their actions will not do them harm. Be prepared to cycle back to providing safety if the child starts to become overwhelmed.

7   Developing social awareness

Help the child to think about the social consequences of the event. Ensure that they have ready personal strategies for positive reintegration with the group. Prepare the child to connect with positive allies who will assist reintegration.

8   Developing reflectivity

Encourage the child to reflect on what they have learned, and how they will take note of putting the learning into practice. Ask them to suggest ways they will notice if they have improved their ability to regulate their behaviour. Check that they have heard and understood positive comments about their courage in dealing with their difficulties.

9   Developing reciprocity

Tell the child what you have learned by working with them on this. Thank them for anything you can thank them for.

2

Article 39 of the United Nations Convention on the Rights of the Child

- **States Parties shall take all appropriate measures to promote physical and psychological recovery and social reintegration of a child victim of:**
    - any form of neglect, exploitation or abuse
    - torture or any other form of cruel, inhuman or degrading treatment or punishment
    - armed conflicts.

- **Such recovery and reintegration shall take place in an environment which fosters the health, self-respect and dignity of the child.**

We are a State, and we are party to the Convention. Therefore it is our duty to treat child victims of trauma properly. Children have a right to be helped to recover.

Part 3
Ideas for using this material

Ideas for using the Powerpoint presentation

The presentation and case studies in this guide can be used as source material for training. Sample programmes may illustrate the variety of possible training opportunities. The following suggestions may prompt your creativity – you can change or adapt all the material to suit the needs of your learning.

One day INSET or care agency training day

Introduction

Introduce trainer/facilitator.

Explain arrangements for day.

Deliver any necessary announcements (fire instructions, messages, etc.).

Discuss confidentiality, safety, comfort, sensitivity of subject matter.

Session 1
Lasting effects of early adversity

- What are the behaviours that most worry us? – reflect in small groups/pairs and list.

- The origins of worrying behaviours – presentation selected from PowerPoint slides and linked to listed behaviours.

Session 2
Secondary effects of early adversity

- Powerful negative feelings generated in us when living and working with traumatised children – reflect individually and list.

- Secondary stress disorders – presentation selected from PowerPoint slides and linked to listed feelings.

- Prevention strategies – reflect individually and then in small groups on personal, social and professional sources of resilience.

Session 3
Living and working with children who have lived through adversity

- Patterns of recovery and adaptation – presentation of the slide showing the nine-point curriculum for effective working.

- A child in mind – small groups discuss current practice and select a child to think about.

- What is most difficult for this child? Groups use course materials to help in selecting no more than three significant current difficulties for the child they are thinking about.

- What is most difficult for us? Groups use course materials to help in selecting no more than three significant current difficulties for the adults who care for the child.

Session 4
Ways forward

- Helping children to recover and adapt – same small groups use course materials to generate ideas for living and working effectively at home and at school with the child being considered. Record results to share with whole group.

- Caring for the carers – small group work applying prevention strategies to maintaining the well-being of those living and working with this child.

- Sharing planning – small group presents to large group brief bullet points showing suggestions for ways forward in helping children to recover and adapt and helping carers to stay well.

Summary and conclusion

Facilitator sums up the day's work and invites comments.

Half-day training

Use EITHER material on long-term effects of early adversity OR secondary effects as starting point for reflective discussion and learning.

Twilight or short evening session

Use individual slides or a few linked slides to prompt reflective discussion and learning.

Individual study

Provide material from the resource guide for individuals to study and think about in their own time, then use this as the basis of a support group or team discussion.

3

As an aid to supervision

Use relevant material from the resource guide to illuminate issues and help planning in supervision.

As a resource for planning and review meetings

Use relevant material to contribute to the planning or review process.

As a resource to inform school policy discussions

Use relevant material to raise teachers' and managers' awareness of issues and how this might affect policies and practice.

As a resource for working directly with children and young people

Adapt material from the resource guide creatively to contribute directly to work with children and young people. Remember that an early step towards recovery and adaptation is the development of some knowledge and understanding of the processes and dynamics that lead to the difficulties the child experiences in self regulation and in making sense of the world.

Tips to enhance learning

- Assume that this material will be personally and emotionally challenging for some people.

- Acknowledge these difficulties openly to participants, while also recognising that we cannot work effectively with traumatised children until we are willing and able to think clearly about their experience.

- Invite participants to take adult responsibility for their own wellbeing while working on these issues.

- Take time to reflect on your own experience in relation to the subject matter.

- Appropriate sharing of personal and professional experience is the best aid to learning in this sensitive subject area. Be prepared to use anecdotes and stories from personal experience of working with traumatised children, within the limits of confidentiality.

- Inappropriate sharing of unprocessed personal experience is, however, a great block to learning. If in doubt, check with a colleague.

- Always, however short the training session, find some time to allow participants to reflect directly on their work, to make connections between the material of the course and their own experience, and to think about ways in which they can apply what they have learned.

Ideas for using the case studies

Certain themes emerge from the case studies that indicate key issues or intervention points. These were: 1) Assessment of need; 2) Planning; 3) Placement stability; 4) Skilled internventions; 5) Caring for carers. During the lengthy piloting of this training material, practitioners have commented on changes they have observed at these key points when this approach is applied. Each of the key points is numbered, with subsections a, b, and c. In each case section (a) relates to the first section of the presentation, and invites the participant to reflect on the ways in which a deeper understanding of the effects of unmet attachment need and early trauma might make a difference to practice in this area. The (b) sections relate to the second section of the presentation, and encourage participants to reflect on the ways in which recognising and understanding the effects of secondary traumatic stress might have an impact on effective practice. And finally the (c) sections suggest reflection on the effects on practice of having an approach to working with traumatised children that expects and promotes recovery and adaptation.

The case studies and this section on revisiting the case studies are included as handouts on the CD ROM. Each case study has these key points listed alongside in boxes, inviting participants to identify from the text the key points at which increased knowledge and understanding might have produced different practice, or points at which practitioners showed skilled work in relation to issues of attachment and trauma. These handouts can be used on their own or together with material from the presentation as an exercise in training or to provide material for discussion groups. An example of a partial analysis is given at the end of this section, along with some brief notes indicating ideas that might emerge from the other case studies.

1 Assessment of need

a) Understanding of issues of attachment and trauma can produce speedier, more child-centred assessments.

b) Understanding of issues of secondary traumatic stress can help in screening out avoidance, in which the child is overlooked or blamed, or panic, in which the child is perceived as unduly dangerous or powerful.

c) Belief in the possibility of recovery or adaptation, and understanding of issues of resilience, can reduce paralysis in the face of apparently intractable situations.

2 Planning

a) Recognition of the disintegrative effects of trauma encourages all those with responsibility for the child to work together to ensure that plans are effective and do not perpetuate the disintegration.

b) Recognition of the power of secondary traumatic stress to create conflict and reduce clear communication between the adults responsible for the child helps workers to stay calm and child centred while producing joined-up planning.

c) Having a model for understanding the process of recovery and adaptation helps set a framework for constructing effective plans for the child.

3   Placement stability

a)   Care families who have been able to make sense of the behaviour of children placed with them in terms of issues of attachment and trauma are more able to survive and thrive.

b)   Social workers, teachers and other professionals who use a model of secondary traumatic stress to make sense of their work with care families are more able to sustain the family placement.

c)   Recognition of the nature and timescales of recovery and adaptation after trauma allows everyone responsible for the welfare of the child to be both more optimistic and more patient.

4   Skilled interventions

a)   Understanding the global nature of developmental and functional impairments after early adversity leads to a recognition that everyone around the child is contributing to the recovery process. This helps people to be motivated to build on their existing skills and to develop appropriate new skills.

b)   Applying the model of secondary traumatic stress promotes understanding of the de-skilling effects of living and working with traumatised children. This in turn leads to better mutual support and more clarity in the use of supervision.

c)   Having a model for the process of recovery and adaptation encourages the development of a range of appropriate skills for helping the child progress on the journey of recovery. It also promotes the recognition of a range of people who may, because of their particular skills, be helpful to the child at different points of the recovery process.

5   Caring for carers

a)   Traumatised children are often exhausting and frustrating people to be with. Everyone who cares for them – care families, teachers, social workers and other people who are part of the care network – may become exhausted and frustrated. Such experiences accumulate: people may become less, not more, effective as they become more experienced. Knowledge and understanding can prevent such burnout.

b)   Secondary traumatic stress can lead to diminished ability to use supervision and support. Knowledgeable supervisors will expect this effect and find ways to continue to support those who care for the child.

c)   Strategies for recovery and adaptation are useful for everyone who ever experiences the symptoms that follow overwhelming stress.

Case study worksheets

An example of a partially annotated worksheet, showing how the case study may be used to contribute to individual learning or group discussions.

POSED BY MODEL

4 John
A 12-year-old boy

John is 12 years old, and is the youngest of four children. The family have been known to social services since the birth of the first child, as the mother is a registered drug user and alcoholic. Their maternal grandmother took on responsibility for maintaining the home as best she could until she became too frail six years ago when John was six years old. When grandmother moved into sheltered housing the family home quickly deteriorated. The children's always sporadic school attendance now stopped completely and a protracted period of frustration for education welfare services and social services ensued. After some six months, entry was forced and inspection revealed the house to be in a state of foul neglect with the children malnourished and infested with lice. Remains of a birthday meal of baked beans was in evidence. Their mother was sectioned under the Mental Health Act and the children were placed in three different foster placements. John and his closest in age sister, who has severe learning difficulties, were separated for the first time.

1a

1b/5a

The two elder girls lived and went to school together but John went alone to his neighbourhood school. While the placements were stable for his siblings, John had problems settling and he developed speech and language difficulties, which manifested themselves as severe stuttering. He found it very difficult to make any significant friendships with peers and was frequently bullied. He withdrew from contact and would spend much of his time at school in tears, making contact only with his education liaison social worker. He was the only one of the children who refused to visit his grandmother, and he cut himself off from family contact.

4a

3a

4a

John was assessed as having complex special educational needs with particular weakness in literacy and organisational skills. No SEN statement was, however, considered necessary.

1b

It was difficult to persuade John to attend school and when he was on site he would often truant from lessons and be found hidden in small spaces. He started to steal from school staff and his carers. Two placements broke down because of the difficulties arising from his challenging behaviour.

When he was 11, John was placed with new carers, with a placement contract providing considerable extra educational input. He was given a place on an out-of-hours "reading for life" scheme run through social services in collaboration with the school; this provides John with access to a computer to use at home. He also has considerable time input from speech therapist. His latest foster placement is in walking distance from his sisters, and he is to join them in attending the same secondary school next year. He has made one visit to see his grandmother. John is beginning to respond positively to this integrated approach to his complex needs.

3

Assessment of need

1a   Earlier intervention could have reduced developmental impairment

1b   Frustration leads to avoidance

1c   Belief in recovery

Planning

2a   Integrated multi0agency approach recognising effects of trauma

2b   Child's behaviour inducing secondary stress leading to breakdown

Placement stability

3a   Stress behaviour of the child partially recognised

3b   Recognition of needs of carers

3c   Ability to partially re-unite siblings starts long road to positive recovery

Skilled interventions

4a   Explicit developmental and functional impairments

4b   Stealing creating secondary stress – deskilling carers

4c   Recognition of the range of interventions

Care of carers

5a   Greater appreciation of effects of exhausting effect on carers can help prevent burnout

Case studies – some suggestions about possible discussion areas

The following are a selection of the kinds of issues that may be raised in discussion groups. They may be helpful in getting people started but are not intended to be definitive.

Susan

'Consistently soiled herself … and was aggressive' – 2a disintegrative effects of trauma

'Significant speech delay' – 2a and 1a issues of attachment needing speedier assessments.

'Exhaustive counselling … began to thrive' – 1c belief in the possibility of recovery reducing paralysis.

'Each placement broke down' – 3a care families not having time to make sense of behaviours so unable to thrive.

'She refused to attend school and became clinically depressed' – 5a issues about the exhaustion of carers caused by secondary trauma. New start sought with different agency.

'Six months of careful work using resources from many agencies' – 4c model for recovery and recognition of the range of skills needed to help that recovery.

'All staff … had agreed, clear responses' – 1a/3c plans and communication allow for patient and optimistic responses.

Andy

'After Andy had been permanently excluded from his Junior School' – 1a assessment focused on child's behaviour rather than on issues of attachment.

'The foster placement rapidly broke down when …' – 4b secondary stress caused by behaviour deskilling both care family and other professionals.

'Taken back into care after assaulting …' – 2a earlier planning may have helped avoid the crisis, disintigrative effect of trauma.

'She moved out herself" – 5b secondary stress leading to inability to access support effectively.

'Consistent schooling was maintained …' – 1c belief in the possibility of adaptation and working together across agencies enabled a period of some stability.

'Flourished in this protected environment …' – 3c a recognition of the timescales for recovery allow for optimism.

Gita

'Two children's homes and five foster placements' – 3b Gita's behaviour created huge tensions in the placements, a clearer understanding of a model of secondary traumatic stress may have helped sustain placements.

'Within three months she was on the verge of being permanently excluded' – 1a understanding of issues relating to bereavement trauma.

'An interagency meeting was called' – 4a attempts to understand the global nature of functional impairments to try to help people to be motivated to build on existing skills.

'The school could not discover her whereabouts' – 5a breakdown in communication between agencies as professionals become more frustrated by the intractable nature of the problems and "burnout".

'Gita was beyond her control' – 5b secondary traumatic stress leading to inability to put plans into action and hopelessness.

'As long as she behaved' – 2a little recognition of the disintegrative effects of trauma and plans based on wishful thinking.

Wayne

'Found unconscious in a pool of blood' – 1a understanding of the issues of trauma.

'For a further year …' – 2c having a model for the process of recovery could have helped set an earlier framework for effective planning.

'Wayne was placed with foster carers' – 1c belief in the possibility of recovery reducing paralysis.

'Produced forged notes' – 4a greater understanding of the global nature of developmental impairments would have helped.

'Wife would not attend' – 5b secondary traumatic stress in carers leading to inability to use support effectively.

'The foster placement broke down' – 5a traumatised children are exhausting and carers can become frustrated and unable to cope.

Kayleigh

'She was an aggressive child and three placements broke down' – 1b greater understanding of secondary stress may have helped in avoidance where the child is perceived as unduly dangerous.

'She would bite and slap' – 2a recognition of the disintegrative effects of trauma helpful in creating long-term plans.

'She was excluded from school' – 3c understanding of timescales of recovery, especially when further trauma experienced, could lead to greater patience.

'But this was rejected for lack of clear evidence' – 4a/4c understanding of global nature of developmental impairments may lead to more wholistic approach by all agencies. Recognition of the range of people helpful to promoting recovery.

'Seeking a new foster placement' – 5c strategies for recovery useful for all who may be connected with Kayleigh in the future.

3

Who's involved with looked after children in education?

At school level

Teachers

Teachers have regular contact with children in care and should be aware, in a general way, of any sensitivities which might affect the behaviours or learning needs of those in their classrooms.

Pastoral staff

Year Heads, Heads of House, Tutors – all have a responsibility for having daily contact with children in care and can provide invaluable feedback about progress.

Designated teacher

Each school should have a teacher with influence over policy-making who is responsible for:

- liaison between agencies involved with all children in care in the school
- provision of appropriate in-school support
- the flow of relevant information both within and between schools
- the maintenance of Personal Education Plans for each child
- acting as an advocate for the child

Special Educational Needs Co-ordinator (SENCO)

Each school has a SENCO who is responsible for ensuring that children with identified special educational needs receive the support necessary for them to access the curriculum.

School nurse

Most schools will have a member of staff with day-by-day responsibility for the physical health of the children. They may act as the point of contact between health professionals and the school.

Beyond the school staff

Educational psychologist

Educational psychologists are consulted by schools, and sometimes by social services, when detailed assessments about learning, emotional and behavioural needs are required. They may be involved at many levels in working with individuals or groups of children, parents and staff.

Education welfare officers

EWOs work with children and parents, usually referred to them by schools, where there are attendance issues affecting the performance of children. They may be involved with a wide range of local programmes in order to help improve school attendance.

Connexions personal advisors

Connexions advisors work closely with schools to provide a range of services for individual children, particularly those who are experiencing problems. They may act as learning mentors, and will provide links to careers guidance services.

LEA "lead officers"

Each local education authority has a senior officer with particular responsibility for oversight of the provision of education for children in care.

Who's involved with looked after children in social care?

Foster carers

Families providing foster care may work for the local authority or for independent fostering providers. They may also be members of the child's own family providing foster care on behalf of the local authority. Foster care provides the child with a family environment with carers who have received training and are supported to promote recovery from trauma.

Residential workers

If the child is in a children's home, they will be cared for by residential workers. Usually the child will have a key worker, who is a named individual with responsibility for working directly with the child and for taking the part of a parent to the child in relation to other agencies such as education and health.

Family placement social workers

Specialist social workers employed by the fostering agency (the local authority or the independent fostering provider) to support and supervise the foster care family. They will be involved from the point of planning the placement in all issues to do with the welfare of the family.

Children's social workers

The social worker for the child has responsibility for assessing the needs of the child and then for planning and supporting the placement. Many local authorities split these tasks, so that one social worker has responsibility for the initial assessment of need, and another social worker takes over long-term responsibility once the child becomes looked after.

Independent reviewing officers

Every child in public care must have a care plan which is reviewed at regular intervals. The review of the care plan will be discussed at a review meeting chaired by the Independent Reviewing Officer.

Educational support workers

Some local authorities, and some independent fostering providers, provide specialist workers to promote the education of the looked after child. These workers may have different titles in different organisations.

3

References

Department for Education and Skills (2003) *Every Child Matters,* London: Department for Education and Skills

Department of Health (1998) *The Government Response to Children's Safeguards Review,* London: Department of Health

Department of Health (1998) *National Priorities Guidance* London: Department of Health

Department of Health (1998) *Quality Protects,* London: Department of Health

Department of Health/Department for Education and Skills (2000) *The Joint Guidance on the Education of Children in Public Care,* London: Department of Health/Department for Education and Skills

Department of Health (2002) *The National Minimum Standards for Children's Homes and Fostering Services,* London: Department of Health

Dixon, B (2003) *Education: A Carer's Handbook,* London: National Teaching and Advisory Service

Fletcher-Campbell, F Archer, T and Tomlinson, K (2003) *The Role of the School in Supporting the Education of Children in Care,* London: National Foundation for Educational Research

Hibbert, H (2003) *Education Matters: For everyone working with children in public care,* London: The Who Cares? Trust

Janoff-Bulman, R (1992) *Shattered Assumptions: Towards a new psychology of trauma,* New York: The Free Press

Social Exclusion Unit (1998) *Truancy and School Exclusion,* London: Social Exclusion Unit

Social Exclusion Unit (2003) *A Better Education for Children in Care,* London: Social Exclusion Unit

SSI/Ofsted (1994) *Education of Children who are Looked After by Local Authorities,* London: SSI/Ofsted

Utting, W (1997) *People Like Us: The report of the review of the safeguards for children living away from home,* London: The Stationery Office

Useful books

APA (1994) *Diagnostic and Statistical Manual of Mental Disorders*, American Psychiatric Association

Bettelheim, B (1974) *A Home for the Heart*, Thames and Hudson

Bowlby, J (1980) *Attachment, Separation and Loss (three volumes)*, London: Penguin

Braithwaite, J (1989) *Crime, Shame and Reintegration*, Cambridge University Press

Bronfenbrenner, U (1979) *The Ecology of Human Development: Experiments by nature and design*, Harvard University Press

Cairns, K (1999) *Surviving Paedophilia: Traumatic stress after organised and network child sexual abuse*, Stoke on Trent: Trentham Books

Cairns, K (2002) *Attachment, Trauma and Resilience: Therapeutic caring for children*, London: BAAF

Carter, R (1998) *Mapping the Mind*, London: Weidenfeld and Nicholson

Coles, R (1986) *The Moral Life of Children*, Boston: Houghton Mifflin

Coles, R (1990) *The Spiritual Life of Children*, Boston: Houghton Mifflin

Csikszentmihalyi, M (1993) *The Evolving Self: A psychology for the third millennium*, London: HarperCollins

Damasio, A (1999) *The Feeling of What Happens: Body, emotion and the making of consciousness*, London: William Heinemann

Daniel, B and Wassell, S (2002) *The Early Years: Assessing and promoting resilience in vulnerable children (1)*, London: Jessica Kingsley

Daniel, B and Wassell, S (2002) *The School Years: Assessing and promoting resilience in vulnerable children (2)*, London: Jessica Kingsley

Daniel, B and Wassell, S (2002) *Adolescence: Assessing and promoting resilience in vulnerable children (3)*, London: Jessica Kingsley

De Zulueta, F (1993) *From Pain to Violence: The traumatic origins of destructiveness*, London: Whurr Publishing

Demos, V (ed.) (1995) *Exploring Affect: The selected writings of Silvan S. Tomkins*, Cambridge University Press

Erikson, H (1963) *Childhood and Society*, New York: Norton

Fahlberg, V (1994) *A Child's Journey Through Placement*, London: BAAF

Figley, C (1995) *Compassion Fatigue: Coping with secondary traumatic stress disorder in those who live with the traumatized*, London: Brunner-Routledge

Gilligan, R (2001) *Promoting Resilience: A resource guide on working with children in the care system*, London: BAAF

Harris-Hendriks, J, Black, D and Kaplan, T (2000) *When Father Kills Mother: Guiding children through trauma and grief*, London: Routledge

Howe, D, Brandon, M, Hinings, D and Schofield, G (1999) *Attachment Theory, Child Maltreatment and Family Support: A practice and assessment model*, Basingstoke: Macmillan

Hughes, D (1997) *Facilitating Developmental Attachment: The road to emotional recovery and behavioural change in foster and adoptive children*, Jason Aronson

Hughes, D (1998) *Building the Bonds of Attachment: Awakening love in deeply troubled children*, Jason Aronson

Jackson, S (ed.) (2001) *Nobody Ever Told Us School Mattered: Raising the educational attainments of children in care*, London: BAAF

Janoff-Bulman, R (1992) *Shattered Assumptions: Towards a new psychology of trauma*, London: The Free Press

Karr-Morse, R and Wiley, M (1997) *Ghosts from the Nursery: Tracing the roots of violence*, Boston: Atlantic Monthly Press

Kaufman, G (1992) *Shame: The power of caring*, Vermont: Schenkman Books

McNamara, J (1995) *Bruised Before Birth: Parenting children exposed to parental substance abuse*, London: BAAF

Richardson, J and Joughin, C (2000) *The Mental Health Needs of Looked After Children*, London: Gaskell

Schofield, G, Beek, M, Sargent, K with Thoburn, J (2000) *Growing Up in Foster Care*, London: BAAF

Shotter, J (1984) *Social Accountability and Selfhood*, Oxford: Basil Blackwell

Strong, M (2000) *A Bright Red Scream: Self-mutilation and the language of pain*, London: Virago Press

Tedeschi, R and Calhoun, G (1995) *Trauma and Transformation: Growing in the aftermath of suffering*, London: Sage

van der Kolk, B, McFarlane, A and Weisaeth, L (eds.) (1996) *Traumatic Stress: The effects of overwhelming experience on mind, body and society*, New York: The Guilford Press

Wilber, K (2000) *Integral Psychology: Consciousness, spirit, psychology, therapy*, Boston: Shambhala Publications

Wolin, S. J and Wolin, S (1993) *The Resilient Self: How survivors of troubled families rise above adversity*, New York: Villard Books